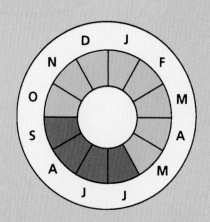

Fruiting Code

One of these symbols is shown with each fungus. The pink segments show you at a glance in which months of the year you will be able to see this fungus because it is the time to fruit (release its spores). In this example, the fungus is fruiting between June and September.

MUSHROOMS & FUNGI

Geoffrey Kibby

EDITED BY
Leslie Jackman

DRAGON'S WORLD

CHILDREN'S BOOKS

Conservation

Because the fungus that you see is only the fruiting body of the main fungus, you will not damage it by picking what you see. It is like picking an apple – that doesn't damage the apple tree. However, you must be careful not to damage the habitat, because the fungus does depend on that. As you learn more about a habitat, you will get to know which fungi you could expect to find there. Before you go walking in the country, make sure you read the Fungi Collector's Code below.

Many habitats have been damaged or destroyed by pollution, agriculture and industry. Some fungi are in danger of disappearing altogether because their habitats have been disturbed or destroyed. On page 78, you will find the names of some societies who campaign for the preservation of habitats and fungi. By joining them and supporting their efforts, you can help to preserve our environment in all its richness and beauty.

Fungi Collector's Code

1 **Always go collecting with a friend,** and always tell an adult where you have gone.
2 **Don't pick more than one specimen.** Leave the rest to make more fungi.
3 **If you are in any doubt** about whether a fungus is poisonous, **DO NOT TOUCH IT.**
4 **Never eat wild fungi** unless they have been checked by an adult who is also a fungi expert.
4 **Ask permission** before exploring or crossing private property.
5 **Keep to footpaths** as much as possible and don't trample the undergrowth.
6 **Keep off crops and leave fence gates** as you find them.

Dragon's World Ltd
Limpsfield
Surrey RH8 0DY
Great Britain

First published by Dragon's World Ltd, 1994

© Dragon's World Ltd, 1994
© Text Dragon's World Ltd, 1994
© Species illustrations Geoffrey Kibby 1992 & 1994
© Other illustrations Dragon's World Ltd, 1994

Simplified text and captions by Leslie Jackman, based on *Mushrooms and Other Fungi of Britain and Northern Europe* by Geoffrey Kibby.

Species illustrations by Geoffrey Kibby. Habitat paintings by Michael Saunders. Headbands by Antonia Phillips. Activities illustrations by Mr Gay Galsworthy.

Editor	Diana Briscoe
Designer	James Lawrence
Design Assistant	Victoria Furbisher
Art Director	John Strange
Editorial Director	Pippa Rubinstein

British Library Cataloguing in Publication Data
The catalogue record for this book is available from the British Library.

ISBN 1 85028 239 0

Typeset in Frutiger Light and Novarese Bold by Dragon's World Ltd.
Printed in Slovenia.

Contents

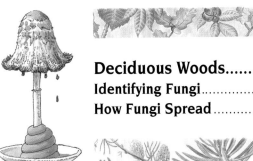

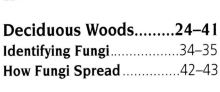

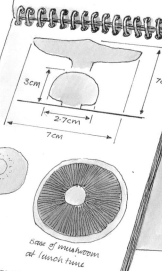

What are Fungi?

The words mushrooms and toadstools mean the same thing. They are the common names given to the larger members of the fungi kingdom. Fungi (singular fungus) are quite different from both plants and animals. They don't have flowers, or leaves, or proper roots, and they fruit (create more small fungi) by scattering their spores (seeds). Fungi also include the moulds that grow on damp walls, yeast which helps to make bread, and the rusts that attack trees and crops.

What you see in a wood or park is only a small part of the real fungus. Most of it consists of a system of almost-invisible threads (called 'mycelium') which run through the soil, wood, or whatever else the fungus grows and feeds on. Because fungi get their food by breaking down other plants or animals, they do best in the autumn and winter. This is when plants, trees, insects and other creatures are dying down, and so the fungus has lots of food and can fruit.

How a gilled mushroom grows

In damp weather, fungi can grow very fast indeed. The fungus shown in these pictures could grow from nothing to fully-open in under twelve hours. To find out more about spores (the seeds), see pages 34–35 and 42–43.

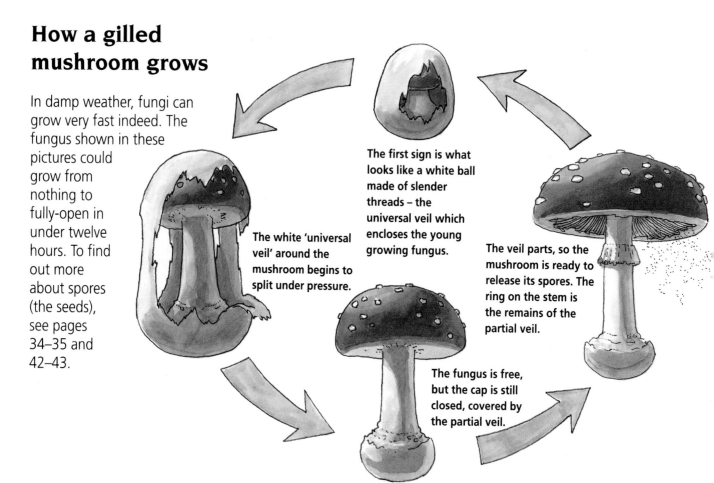

The white 'universal veil' around the mushroom begins to split under pressure.

The first sign is what looks like a white ball made of slender threads – the universal veil which encloses the young growing fungus.

The veil parts, so the mushroom is ready to release its spores. The ring on the stem is the remains of the partial veil.

The fungus is free, but the cap is still closed, covered by the partial veil.

Danger!

Many species of fungi are **poisonous**. You should **never** eat wild mushrooms or fungi, unless they have been checked by an adult who is a expert on fungi.

All the poisonous fungi in this book are identified by the **red** skull and crossbones symbol shown here. If you see one, take a photo or make a drawing of it, but **do not touch it**. If you do touch one, wash your hands carefully as soon as possible.

Possibly poisonous fungi are identified with a **blue** skull and crossbones – avoid touching them.

Habitat Picture Bands

This book is divided into different habitats (or type of countryside). Each habitat has a different picture band at the top of the page. These are shown below.

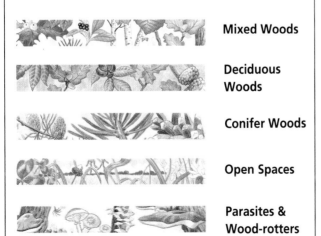

Mixed Woods

Deciduous Woods

Conifer Woods

Open Spaces

Parasites & Wood-rotters

How to use this book

There are well over 2,000 species of fungi to be found across Europe in every possible type of habitat. Because fungi are not as popular as plants or animals, many of them only have a scientific Latin name. Where there is an English name as well, you will find it at the start of the entry.

When trying to identify a fungus – for example the red or yellow ones below, follow these steps.

1 **Decide what habitat you are in**. If you aren't sure, read the descriptions at the start of each section to see which one fits best. Each habitat has a different picture band heading and these are shown below.

2 **What colour is your fungus?** Look at the pages of fungi which are this colour in the habitat you just have identified. The information and pictures given will help you to name it. The red fungus (above) is a *Boletus rubellus* (see page 31). There is more on how to identify fungi on pages 34–35.

3 **If you can't find the fungus**, look through the other sections. Parasites are in a different section. You will find the yellow fungus (below) on page 69. It is a *Sparassis crispa*.

4 **If you still can't find the fungus,** you may have to look in a larger field guide (see page 78 for some suggestions). You might have spotted something very rare or even unknown!

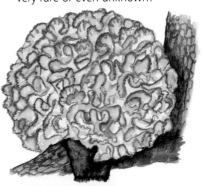

What To Look For

Gilled Mushrooms

Some have stems and others grow from trees like a shelf, but they all have gills containing spores. They are the ones you are most likely to find.

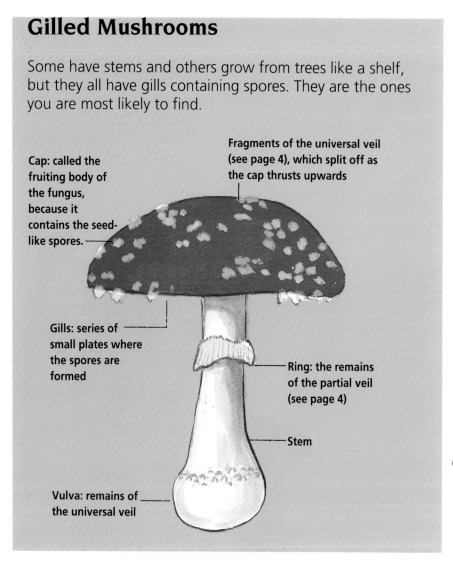

Cap: called the fruiting body of the fungus, because it contains the seed-like spores.

Fragments of the universal veil (see page 4), which split off as the cap thrusts upwards

Gills: series of small plates where the spores are formed

Ring: the remains of the partial veil (see page 4)

Stem

Vulva: remains of _____ the universal veil

Chantarelles

Similar to gilled mushrooms, but they have blunt-edged wrinkles instead of gills under the cap. Some are trumpet-shaped and almost smooth on the outside.

Toothed Fungi

Some have caps and stems, others grow out of trees like a shelf. They all have downward pointing teeth or spines under the cap where the spores form.

Tubed Mushrooms or Boletes

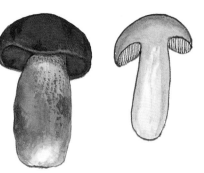

Similar to gilled mushrooms, but they have spongy tubes with open ends under the cap.

Puffballs, Earthstars & Bird's Nests

These fungi have no gills and no pores – a ball-like structure contains the spores. It explodes when the spores are ripe.

Stinkhorns

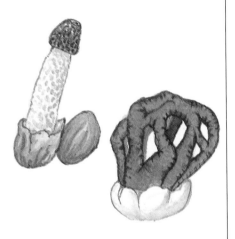

These fungi 'hatch' from an egg and the spores are spread over special structures. The spores liquefy and produce a foul smell which attracts flies. The flies then collect and disperse the spores.

Polypores, Bracket & Crust Fungi

Most grow on trees. They usually have one or more layers of downward pointing tubes on the underside. Some crust fungi do not have a tube layer.

Club & Coral Fungi

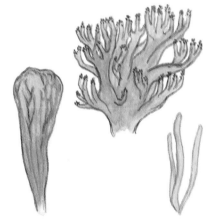

These range from the simplest club-shaped fruiting bodies to complex coral-like forms. The spores are produced over most of the surface of the clubs.

Jelly Fungi

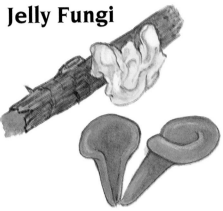

They vary in form and size from minute blobs of shapeless jelly to ones shaped like ears or tongues. All are soft and jelly-like or sometimes rubbery.

Morels, False Morels & Cup Fungi

These range from microscopic-sized to brain-like or sponge-like structures on a stem, usually brittle in texture. The spores are held in cylindrical cells (called 'ascus'), which are usually spread over the cup surface or are held in pits in the sponge-like forms. The spores are ejected in a dust cloud when it is disturbed.

Mixed Woodlands

Mixed woodlands describes a wood or forest where you find broad-leaf trees (ones with broad, flat leaves) growing alongside conifers (trees with needles instead of leaves). Most broad-leaf trees are deciduous, which means that they lose their leaves in the autumn and survive the harsh winter weather with bare branches. Both sorts of tree grow all over Britain.

As you will see in later habitats, there are many fungi that only grow on or near a particular type of tree, like a beech or a pine. They live in a sort of partnership with the tree – the fungus gets food from the tree's roots, and the tree gets elements that it can't get otherwise from the fungus.

However, there are also many fungi that will grow in partnership with a number of different tree species. If you are hunting fungi in a mixed wood, you should look very carefully at what trees are around you. If you find a fungus in the middle of a group of silver birches, for example, you may need to look in the **Deciduous Woods** section, because it is a fungus that only grows with birches. If the fungus is growing on a dead log, you may have to look in the **Parasites & Wood-rotters** section.

The picture shows fourteen fungi from the following section; how many can you identify?

Amanita pantherina, Amanita spissa, Boletus badius, Boletus chrysenteron, Boletus edulis, Boletus erythropus, Cantharellus cibarius, Collybia maculata, Laetiporus sulphureus, Leccinum holopus, Mycena galopus, Piptoporus betulinus, Russella cyanoxantha, Thelephora terrestris.

Mixed Woodlands

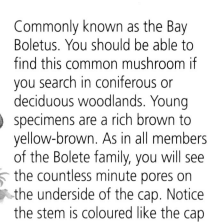

Boletus badius

Commonly known as the Bay Boletus. You should be able to find this common mushroom if you search in coniferous or deciduous woodlands. Young specimens are a rich brown to yellow-brown. As in all members of the Bolete family, you will see the countless minute pores on the underside of the cap. Notice the stem is coloured like the cap with pinkish-brown tones. Some have a whitish-bloom. The whitish-yellow flesh bruises pale blue.

Bolete family
Cap size: 5–10 cm
Spore print colour: Olive-brown
Smell: Mushroom-like
Season: Late summer to early winter

Boletus edulis

Commonly known as the Cep or Penny Bun, this mushroom's cap resembles a brown bun. Usually smooth and dry although its colour can vary from yellow-brown to deep reddish-brown. Its habitat is coniferous, deciduous and mixed woodlands. Like all members of the Bolete family the underside of the cap is sponge-like due to the massed tiny pores. In the Cep, these are off-white to yellow-olive. If you look closely, you will see that the upper stem is covered in a fine network of white ridges.

Bolete family
Cap size: 10–25 cm
Spore print colour: Olive brown
Smell: Pleasant
Season: Late summer to early winter

Boletus chrysenteron

This mushroom is common in mixed woods. It is fairly easy to recognize as its olive-brown to reddish-brown cap is often cracked, revealing its reddish flesh. The pores under the cap are yellow. When bruised they turn blue. The top part of the slender stem is yellowish-white shading to purplish-red lower down.

Bolete family
Cap size: 5–8 cm
Spore print colour: Bronze-olive
Smell: Slightly pleasant
Season: Autumn

Boletus erythropus

Search for this mushroom in mixed woodland. Its pores, which are usually a deep, almost blood-red, change to a more orange colour in cold weather. When you find one, examine the yellowish-orange stem with your hand-lens. If it is overlaid with very fine red dots it may well be this species. Another test is to cut the flesh, which should flush a deep blue.

Bolete family
Cap size: 5–15 cm
Spore print colour: Olive-bronze
Smell: Not very distinctive
Season: July to early winter

Boletus piperatus

Commonly known as the Peppery Boletus. Many fungi are to be found in close association with trees and other features of the habitat. This one is common under birch trees and close to the Fly Agaric (*Amanita muscaria*, see page 33). You will frequently find mushrooms of the Bolete family and others with pieces eaten out of them. This is the work of slugs and snails, the latter numbering over forty species in some woods. The Peppery Boletus has an orange-brown cap and the base of the stem is always a bright chrome-yellow.

Bolete family
Cap size: 3–8 cm
Spore print colour: Brown
Smell: Not particularly distinctive
Season: Late summer to early winter

Tylopilus felleus

Commonly known as the Bitter Bolete. You need to be careful not to confuse this one with the Cep (*Boletus edulis,* see opposite). Note the difference in the stem. The Bitter Bolete has a stem covered in a coarse brown network whereas the stem of the Cep is covered in fine white ridges. The habitat of the Bitter Bolete is under mixed deciduous trees, especially beech and oak. The cap is brown and slightly downy at first but becomes smooth with age.

Bolete family
Cap size: 5–20 cm
Spore print colour: Pinkish to purplish
Smell: A little unpleasant
Season: August to autumn

Russula nigricans

Commonly known as the Black Russula. This gilled mushroom is common in mixed woodlands. The cap starts white and rounded, and ages to a funnel shape. The gills are very thick and widely spaced. Between some of them are shorter gills. If you expose the white flesh, you will find it turns red then black. A good time to look for this species is after heavy rain in mid summer. You may come across a circle of old specimens looking as if they have all been burnt, but this is due to the colour change that takes place with age.

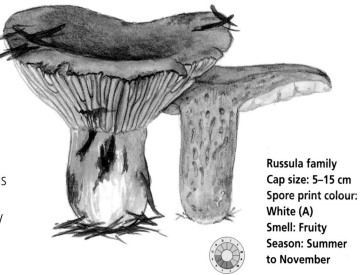

Russula family
Cap size: 5–15 cm
Spore print colour: White (A)
Smell: Fruity
Season: Summer to November

Mixed Woodlands

Lactarius rufus

Commonly known as the Rufus Milk-cap. You will find this fungus in a number of habitats. Pine and birch are good places to search, and it usually prefers boggy areas. The cap is a deep fox or brick red and it has a sharp central umbo (bump). The stem is a similar colour but is white near the base. Like all the *Lactarius* mushrooms it gives off droplets of latex from its gills or flesh when damaged.

Russula family
Cap size: 5–10 cm – Spore print colour: Cream
Smell: None – Season: Summer and autumn

Lactarius camphoratus

Commonly known as the Curry Milk-cap. You will possibly recognize this member of the family by its smell rather than appearance. Its smell of curry becomes stronger as the mushroom ages. The latex it gives off is watery white but rather scarce. It is a common species throughout Britain both under pines and in mixed woodland. The cap and stem are reddish-brown to liver colour and the cap has a small umbo at its centre.

Russula family
Cap size: 2.5–5 cm
Spore print colour: Yellowish
Smell: Curry
Season: Late summer to late autumn

Collybia butyracea

Commonly known as the Butter Cap, the name *butyracea* means buttery or greasy and refers to the texture of the cap surface. In humid weather, it becomes very slippery and greasy to the touch. The gills are very crowded and often jagged at the edges. It changes colour from dark brown to cream colour with age. Search for it beneath pines, although occasionally it is found under deciduous trees too. It grows in troops across the needle litter where it may be quite common.

Tricholoma family
Cap size: 5–7.5 cm
Spore print colour: Cream-buff
Smell: Possibly mushroomy
Season: Autumn

Amanita rubescens

Commonly known as the Blusher. This is another species for you to look at but not touch. You might discover it in deciduous or coniferous woodland where it is sometimes quite common. The name 'Blusher' refers to the flush of pinkish-red which appears in the flesh when it is damaged. All parts eventually became a dull reddish colour. When young, the cap may be almost white, pale yellowish-brown to almost pink. It will be spotted with wart-like pieces of white veil.

Amanita family
Cap size: 5–15 cm
Spore print colour: White
Smell: Avoid smelling it
Season: Summer and autumn
POISONOUS

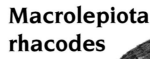

Amanita pantherina

Commonly known as the Panther Cap. This is a very poisonous species, causing delirium, vomiting and a coma-like sleep. On rare occasions it can cause death. Its pale grey-brown to dark brown cap is strikingly sprinkled with pure white warty fragments of veil. Look carefully at the stem and you will see it has a round bulb at the base and one or more narrow rings of veil just above. This fungus is uncommon in mixed woodland. ☠

Amanita family
Cap size: 5–10 cm – Spore print colour: White
Smell: Avoid smelling it – Season: Late summer into autumn
POISONOUS

Amanita fulva

Commonly known as Tawny Grisette. This is one of the commonest species in Britain and can be found in most woodlands. Its cap ranges from orange-brown to reddish-brown. If you look near the base of the cream stem you will see a bag which is the remains of the veil. There are over twenty species of the *Amanita* family in Britain. But beware, it contains some of the most beautiful and most deadly mushrooms in the world.

Amanita family
Cap size: 5–10 cm
Spore print colour: White
Smell: Not distinctive
Season: Late summer and autumn

Macrolepiota rhacodes

This species comes in two varieties, which are sometimes regarded as two species. The picture shows the typical variety you will find in woodlands. It grows on deep leaf litter or needle beds in conifer woods. You may find the second much larger variety on a compost heap or leaf bed. The flesh of both bruises reddish-brown.

Lepiota family
Cap size: 7.5–15 cm
Spore print colour: White – Smell: Pleasantly scented
Season: Throughout summer to late autumn

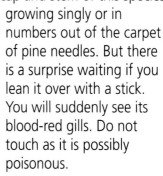

Cortinarius semisanguineus

If you search in birch or pine woods you may see the yellow-brown silky cap and stem of this species growing singly or in numbers out of the carpet of pine needles. But there is a surprise waiting if you lean it over with a stick. You will suddenly see its blood-red gills. Do not touch as it is possibly poisonous.

Cortinarius family
Cap size: 2.5–5 cm
Spore print colour: Rust-brown
Smell: Not distinctive
Season: Late summer to autumn

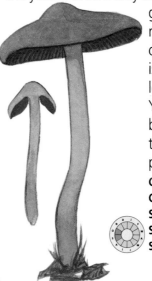

Mycena galopus

This tiny species has a little bell-shaped, grey-brown cap. If you look closely you will see that it is attached to small pieces of wood or leaves in coniferous and mixed woods everywhere. The hollow stem is grey-brown to reddish-brown and has a hairy base. When broken, it drips latex. Although it is so small, you should have no difficulty in finding this species.

Tricholoma family
Cap size: 0.6–1 cm
Spore print colour: White
Smell: None
Season: Summer to autumn

Russula cyanoxantha

The cap colour of this mushroom varies from pure lavender to pure green, or can be a mixture of both. Rub the crowded gills. If you find them soft, flexible and greasy, you have probably found this mushroom. It is found in a wide variety of habitats from conifers to deciduous woodland. Look for it under beech or oak. Whenever you discover a mushroom that interests you, take a very close look at its habitat. Many of them show a marked preference for certain trees, soil condition and presence or absence of other plants.

Russula family
Cap size: 5–15 cm
Spore print colour: White (A)
Smell: No distinctive scent
Season: July to late autumn

Cortinarius purpurascens

Another member of the largest family of mushrooms in the world. Search in a mixed woodland to find this mushroom's sticky, dark brown cap streaked with purple-violet. If it has been damaged you will see a deep purple bruise. Young specimens have cobweb-like strands around the gills, which are common to all *Cortinarius* species.

Cortinarius family
Cap size: 5–10 cm
Spore print colour: Rust-brown
Smell: None
Season: Autumn

Helvella lacunosa

Commonly known as the Black Helvella. The cap of this strange-looking fungus is shaped like a tiny grey-black saddle. It is curled down over the grey and twisted stem, fluted with ribs and pits. It is hollow and has chambers inside. You should be able to recognize it at once as you walk through a mixed woodland. It grows on the track and on mossy banks, and even on burnt soil.

Cup fungus family
Fruit body size: 5–10 cm
Spore print colour: Pale cream
Smell: No distinct odour.
Season: Late summer to autumn

Thelephora terrestris

Commonly known as the Earth Fan, this is one of the Fan Fungi, a group of dark, fleshy, fan-shaped, encrusting species. This one grows against the ground in a fan-shaped dark-brown to grey-brown rosette. You should be able to find it in any mixed woodland. Look for a fungus hugging the soil.

Fan Fungi family
Cap size: 2.5-7.5 cm
Spore print colour:
Purplish-brown
Smell: Earthy, mouldy
Season: Summer to
early winter

Amanita porphyria

You will be lucky to find this one because it is rather uncommon. Where it does grow, its habitat is both coniferous and mixed woods. Notice the large rounded bulb at the base of the stem, and the ring left by the veil high up the stem.

Amanita family
Cap size: 2.5–7.5 cm
Spore print colour: White
Smell: A weak potato or radish scent
Season: Autumn

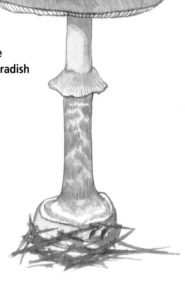

Amanita spissa

Different experts often give different names to some species. This is because new information is constantly being gathered. This one for instance, is also known as *Amanita excelsa*. Young specimens have the grey or brownish cap covered with white patches of volva looking like hoar frost. The stem is bulbous and covered with woolly scaling with a white ring near the top. It is very common in mixed woodland. But beware, as it is easy to confuse this species with the dangerous Panther Cap (*Amanita pantherina*, see page 13), so be careful and do not touch.

Amanita family
Cap size: 5–15 cm
Spore print colour:
White
Smell: Distinctive odour
of potato or radish
Season: Early summer
to late autumn
POISONOUS

Mixed Woodlands

Phallus impudicus

Commonly known as the Stinkhorn, this species has a putrid odour. As you approach you may suspect a dead animal or even the sewage system. This unpleasant smell attracts flies, other insects and slugs which eat the spores and spread them in their droppings. It is common everywhere, even in gardens. Their tough white mycelial cords have been traced through a woodland, moving from stump to stump, often for hundreds of metres. In this way, scores of old stumps become infected.

Stinkhorn family
Cap size: No cap, fungus is 4-6 in (xx cm)tall
Spore print colour: olive
(will not make a spore print)
Smell: Unpleasant, putrid
Season: June-October

Clitopilus prunulus

Commonly known as the Miller. The best clue to this species is its scent. It has a strong, almost pungent smell of fresh-ground meal, or some say cucumber. The white cap has the texture of soft leather and its edge is rolled in. You can see the shape of the gills in the picture. They start white and become pink as the fungus ages. The short stem is often offset from the centre. You will find it in mixed woods everywhere.

Entoloma family
Cap size: 2.5–7.5 cm
Spore print colour: Pink
Smell: Fresh-ground meal or cucumber
Season: Summer and autumn

Russula fragilis

Commonly known as the Fragile Russula. Although this is one of the commonest species of *Russula* in Britain, its colour may present you with a problem, as it is so variable. The cap ranges from purple to red, green, pink or almost black, or mixtures of all of these colours. But with your hand-lens you should be able to sort it out if you take a close look at the white gills. If they are minutely serrated along the edge then your specimen is probably *Russula fragilis*. One more clue, is that the centre of the cap in single colour forms is usually greenish-grey to black.

Russula family
Cap size: 1.5–5 cm
Spore print colour: White (A–B)
Smell: Possibly fruity
Season: Autumn

Clitocybe odora

Commonly known as the Aniseed Cap, this beautiful mushroom advertizes itself with a strong scent of aniseed. As you walk through a wood you may detect it from some distance away. Also you will quickly recognize its delicate blue-green colour. Even the spore colour is unusual as you will see below.

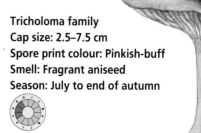

Tricholoma family
Cap size: 2.5–7.5 cm
Spore print colour: Pinkish-buff
Smell: Fragrant aniseed
Season: July to end of autumn

Helvella crispa

Commonly known as White Helvella. A lovely species with a snow-white to cream saddle-shaped cap. Do not confuse it with *Helvella lacunosa* (page 14) which is black. *Helvella crispa* has a white fluted and hollow stem. Look for it in mixed woodlands where it is widespread. You will almost certainly recognize it as a *Helvella* because of its attractive and unusual shape. When out on a fungus foray there is always a new shape, a new colour or a new species for you to discover.

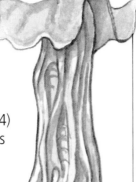

Cup Fungi family
Fruit body size: 2.5–10 cm – Spore print colour: Cream
Smell: Quite pleasant – Season: Autumn

Russula delica

Look for this one under deciduous trees in mixed woodland. It bursts up through the leaf litter after developing underground. It is all white and soon becomes funnel-shaped. The crowded gills sometimes have a bluish tint. You should compare the picture of *Russula delica* with that of *Lactarius vellereus* (see right), because you could confuse the two. However *Russula delica* does not give off latex drops while *Lactarius vellereus* does.

Russula family
Cap size: 7.5–15 cm
Spore print colour:
White to pale cream (A-C)
Smell: Starts fruity, then fishy
Season: Autumn

Boletus calopus

A beautiful Bolete with a rose-red to crimson stem which has a fine white network around it. If damaged, the flesh bruises a pale blue colour. The cap is yellow-brown to whitish-olive. Like other members of the family, they share the layer of minute pores below the cap. You will need to search thoroughly under beech or pine because although widespread it is seldom common.

Bolete family
Cap size: 7.5–20 cm
Spore print colour: Light brown
Smell: Strong and pleasant
Season: Summer and autumn

Lactarius vellereus

You may be surprised by the size of the huge fruiting bodies of this species. Some grow to 20 cm across. This white to ivory velvety cap soon becomes deeply funnel-shaped. In young specimens the cap is tightly rolled up, but it soon unrolls. It cracks in hot weather and releases many drops of very sticky white latex. You will see that the thick gills are quite widely spaced. Despite its size, the hard stem is short, white and velvety. Look for it in mixed woods.

Russula family
Cap size: 8–20 cm
Spore print colour: Buff
Smell: Not noticeable
Season: Late summer and autumn

Mixed Woodlands

Amanita citrina

Commonly known as the False Death Cap, you could mistake this species for the true Death Cap (*Amanita phalloides*, page 26). The gills beneath *Amanita citrina* smell strongly of freshly dug potato which helps to distinguish it. Patches of white veil pattern the cap. It is a very common species throughout Britain and you will find it growing in deciduous, coniferous and mixed woodland. If you think you have found one, look and leave it alone, in case you are mistaken.

Amanita family
Cap size: 5–10 cm
Spore print colour: White
Smell: Freshly dug potatoes
Season: Late summer to autumn

Cantharellus cibarius

Commonly known as the Chanterelle, this species is fairly common in some places where it is to be seen under oaks, birch, beech or pine. It does not have true gills, but if you look carefully under the cap you will see it has many gill-like ridges. The spores are produced on these ridges. It is rather funnel shaped and yellow-orange in colour. Do not confuse it with the False Chanterelle (*Hygrophoropsis aurantiaca*, see opposite).

Chanterelle family
Cap size: 2.5–15 cm
Spore print colour: Pale buff
Smell: A wonderful aroma of apricots
Season: Early summer to late autumn

Leotia lubrica

Commonly known as Jelly Babies, because of its shape, this fungus must not be eaten! It has a rounded, rather rubbery-jelly cap coloured ochre to slightly greenish. If you look closely you will see the yellow-orange stem has darker greenish dots or granules. You will find it growing in small clusters in leaf-litter in mixed woods. Other species have deep olive or blackish-green caps.

Cup Fungi family
Fruit body size: 2.5–5 cm
Spore print colour: White (no spore print possible)
Smell: None
Season: Late summer to autumn

Clavulina cristata

This densely clustered and branched white fungus resembles undersea corals. The colour can vary to cream or yellowish. It is common and you may find it in mixed woods everywhere. A very similar species, *Clavulina cinerea*, has greyish branches with blunt tips, although this can vary. If you walk through a conifer wood, you may see a third related species, *Clavulina rugosa*, which has irregular dirty white branches. Try to find all three of these unusual fungi.

Clavaria family (Club Fungi)
Cap size: 2.5–7.5 cm
Spore print colour: White
Smell: None
Season: Summer to early winter

Hygrophoropsis aurantiaca

Commonly known as the False Chanterelle. You could easily confuse this species with the true Chanterelle (*Cantharellus cibarius*, see opposite). But look closely to spot some differences. The False Chanterelle has true gills which are forked and rather blunt and it does not smell of apricots. This mushroom is very common in mixed woods and heaths throughout Britain. It prefers a damp habitat. The soft, slight velvety yellow-orange cap is thin fleshed with a grooved margin.

Tricholoma family
Cap size: 2.5–7.5 cm – Spore print colour: White
Smell: None obvious – Season: Mid summer to autumn
POSSIBLY POISONOUS

Collybia maculata

This mushroom's common name, Cocoa Caps, comes from the cocoa-coloured spots and stains which soon spread over the once white cap and even on to the stem. It is a common species. If you search carefully over the leaf litter in a beech or conifer wood you may find them forming a fairy ring. If not in a ring, you may find them forming a cluster or 'troop'.

Tricholoma family
Cap size: 5–10 cm
Spore print colour: Pale pinkish buff
Smell: No recognizable scent – Season: Summer and autumn

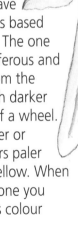

Tricholoma sejunctum

This is a very variable species. Experts have described a number of different varieties based mainly on colour or habitat differences. The one illustrated here is common in both coniferous and deciduous woodlands. But they vary from the common yellow-green to olive-grey with darker fibres like the spokes of a wheel. Others are browner or greener, others paler and almost yellow. When you discover one you should note down its colour pattern and habitat.

Tricholoma family
Cap size: 5–10 cm
Spore print colour: White
Smell: Flour
Season: August-November

Collybia dryophila

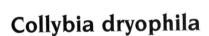

As with all living plants and animals, some species are amazingly successful. This one is certainly a contender for the title of commonest mushroom. It is found all over the temperate regions of the world in a wide variety of habitats. It does, however, show a particular preference for oak and pine. So it could be one of your first trophies. The smooth orange-brown stem has white hairs at the base.

Tricholoma family
Cap size: 2.5–7.5 cm
Spore print colour: Pale cream
Smell: None noticeable
Season: Late spring

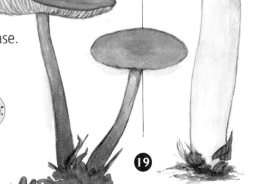

Wet Mixed Woodlands

Cortinarius trivialis

Many *Cortinarius* species prefer damp or wet habitats and this one is no exception. It is usually found in willow bogs. Remember, however, that boggy ground can be dangerous so only search there if you have an adult with you. This species has a sticky, yellow-brown cap with pale lilac gills which on maturity turn rust-brown with spores. The stem is strangely banded with sticky rings of whitish-yellow veil.

Cortinarius family
Cap size: 5–10 cm
Spore print colour: Rust-brown
Smell: None noticeable
Season: Autumn

Leccinum holopus

You will find white members of the Bolete family fairly easy to sort out. To start with, they are rather rare and other Boletes are mostly coloured. *Leccinum holopus* likes a wet habitat, often in sphagnum bogs under birch. The best places to find them are in Scotland and northern England, although they can be found in the south. This fungus starts life pure white but changes to a delicate blue-green with age. The stem flesh often shows a blue-green stain.

Bolete family
Cap size: 5–10 cm
Spore print colour: White to buff
Smell: None
Season: Autumn

Tricholoma fulvum

Here is an easy species to identify. There are other reddish-brown species, but this one is unique in having yellowish, brown-spotted gills. Also if you gently split the brown stem with your fingernail, you will find its flesh is yellow. You will also find the cap is sticky in wet weather. It is a good example of a species growing in close association with a tree, which in this case is the birch in boggy conditions.

Tricholoma family
Cap size: 5–10 cm
Spore print colour: White
Smell: None
Season: Autumn to early winter

Cantharellus tubaeformis

Not as well-known as the Chanterelle (*Cantharellus cibarius*), this fungus is equally common. Compare this picture with *cibarius* on page 18. You will see that this species has a yellow-brown cap which has a very wavy edge. Its undersurface turns colour from yellow to greyish-violet and runs down the stem. The stem is yellow-orange. It grows on acid soils in swampy mixed woodland and also coniferous woodland.

Chanterelle family
Cap size: 2.5–7.5 cm
Spore print colour: Cream
Smell: Aromatic
Season: Mid summer to early winter

Entoloma nidorosum

You may be surprised to know that a number of mushroom species give off a chemical scent like that from a swimming pool. You will find this species smells very strongly. It grows in wet, almost boggy, habitats in woodland, under willow and birch, which often give a clue to boggy ground. The greyish-yellow cap has whitish-grey to pink gills.

Entoloma family
Cap size: 5–7.5 cm
Spore print colour: Pink
Smell: Bleach
Season: Late summer and autumn

Russula caroflava

This species presents one of the brightest caps of any mushroom in the woods. You should be able to spot its vivid yellow colour in the wet or boggy places under birch trees. This is its habitat, and it grows in sphagnum moss. If you scratch it you will find it has turned very slowly to a blackish colour. This species is to be found across the whole of the north temperate regions of the world.

Russula family
Cap size: 5–10 cm
Spore print colour: Pale ochre
Smell: None recognizable
Season: Autumn, or sometimes earlier

Russula emetica

Commonly known as the Sickener. Beware of this fungus. Look, note it down in your field notebook, but do not touch it. It is to be found in wet and boggy pine woods where it grows among sphagnum moss. It has a brilliant scarlet to cherry-red cap. Red is often a warning colour in nature. *Russula emetica* is sticky in wet weather. The gills and stem are pure white, the stem often long and fragile and sometimes swollen towards the base.

Russula family
Cap size: 5–7.5 cm
Spore print colour: White (A)
Smell: Faintly fruity or of coconut
Season: Summer and autumn
POISONOUS ☠

Go on a Fungi Hunt

Hunting for mushrooms and fungi in the wild is great fun, and once you know when and where to look, you'll soon become good at spotting them. You can find mushrooms all year round, but the best time to find them is early morning in the autumn, when there are lots of different kinds.

An important thing to remember about collecting fungi is that some species are poisonous, and it is quite easy to confuse two different species that look similar. So always go mushroom hunting with someone who knows a lot about fungi.

When you collect fungi, only pick one specimen – leave the rest to make spores and more fungi. Something else to remember is that some fungi are very fragile. If you want to take any home, you must be careful about how you transport them.

What you need

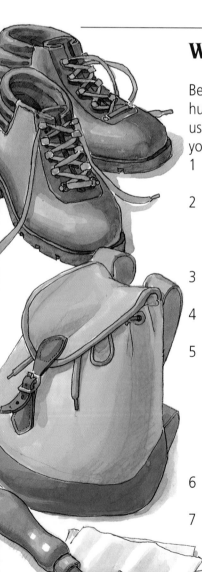

Before you set off on a fungi hunt, gather together a few useful items. Here is a list of what you will need:

1. **A lightweight backpack** to carry everything in.
2. **Rubber boots, walking boots or trainers** (laced up properly) to protect your ankles.
3. **A small trowel** or teaspoon to collect specimens carefully.
4. **A penknife** for cutting specimens. Be careful!
5. **A small magnifying glass:** buy one that is ten power (labelled x 10), and wear it on a cord round your neck. To use it, hold the glass close to your eye and then bring the specimen close to the glass.
6. **Greaseproof or brown paper** for specimens.
7. **Plastic containers or bags** for carrying specimens.

Looking for clues

If you go looking for fungi after it has been raining, see if you can spot any slugs or snails on some of them. You will probably find at least one mushroom that has been nibbled. You may even see some being eaten. If you find a mushroom filled with lots of tiny holes, this is a sign that fly larvae (maggots) have been eating it. Which fungi are eaten by which creatures.

8. **A field notebook, a small box of coloured pencils** or crayons for sketching and biros for making notes.
9. **A camera:** if you take photographs of fungi (particularly those growing on trees), rather than prying them out of the trunk, it avoids damaging the environment.

Carrying specimens home

Some fungi are easily damaged because they are so delicate. When you collect a fungus, handle it carefully and try not to leave any of the stem behind. If you don't wrap specimens carefully, you may find that they have broken when you arrive home. It is important to keep them in good condition so that you can study them properly.

1 **Wrap each specimen separately** in a piece of stiff paper to transport them safely.

2 **Twist the ends of the wrapper** like a sweet paper, then place the package in a plastic container, and put it in your basket or backpack.

3 **Never put unwrapped fungi in a plastic bag.** The bag will mist up and the fungi may get soggy.

What grows where?

Try to find a quiet area of woodland or parkland where you can observe the different kinds of fungi that grow there. Ask an adult to help you choose a suitable spot and mark out an area in the shape of a square. Place stones or sticks at each corner of the area. Now make a careful note of nearby landmarks, like large trees, so that you can find the place again.

Return to your square at different times of the year to see which species of fungi are growing there and how many there are. Make sketches or photograph some of the fungi that you see – for example, a bracket fungus growing on a tree trunk, or a group of mushrooms growing together. Remember to write down exactly when and where you saw them in your field notebook.

Recording your findings

When you pick a mushroom always note the habitat carefully in your field notebook:

- Is the area open or wooded?
- Which kinds of tree grow there?
- Is the fungus growing in a group or on its own?
- Make a note of its colour, shape and texture.
- Is the cap or the stem sticky?
- Does either change colour when you cut it?

If you are taking the specimen home, it is a good idea to write a number on its paper wrapper and put the same number beside your notes and sketches so that you know which fungi is which.

When you get home, keep a permanent record in a ring binder. Have a separate page for each species and stick on to it your most useful notes, sketches and any photographs that you have taken.

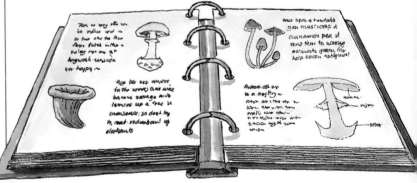

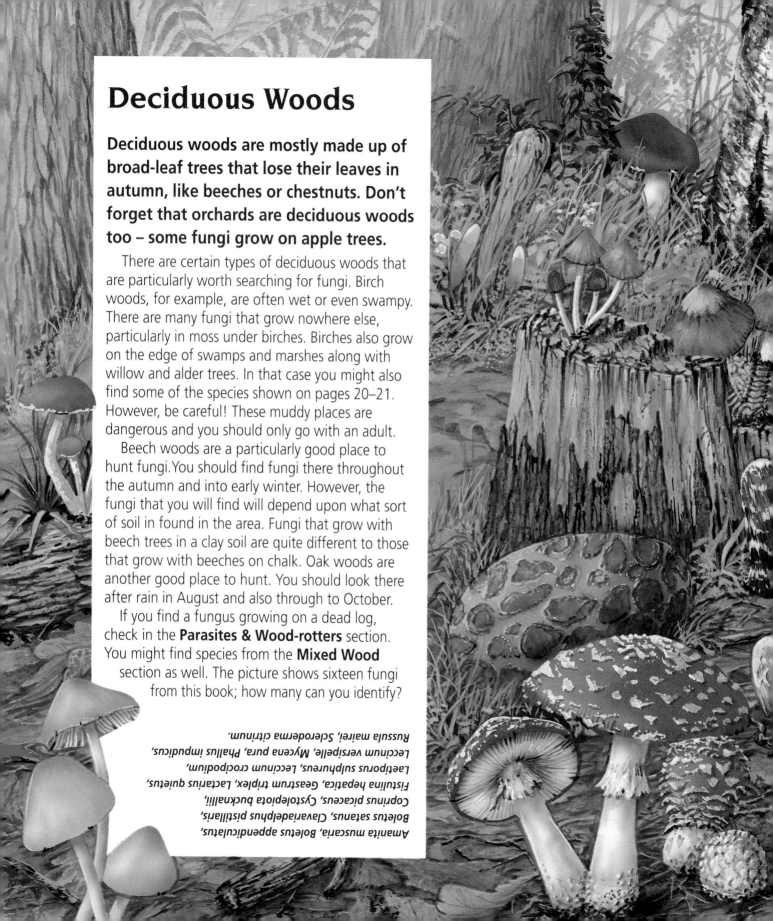

Deciduous Woods

Deciduous woods are mostly made up of broad-leaf trees that lose their leaves in autumn, like beeches or chestnuts. Don't forget that orchards are deciduous woods too – some fungi grow on apple trees.

There are certain types of deciduous woods that are particularly worth searching for fungi. Birch woods, for example, are often wet or even swampy. There are many fungi that grow nowhere else, particularly in moss under birches. Birches also grow on the edge of swamps and marshes along with willow and alder trees. In that case you might also find some of the species shown on pages 20–21. However, be careful! These muddy places are dangerous and you should only go with an adult.

Beech woods are a particularly good place to hunt fungi. You should find fungi there throughout the autumn and into early winter. However, the fungi that you will find will depend upon what sort of soil in found in the area. Fungi that grow with beech trees in a clay soil are quite different to those that grow with beeches on chalk. Oak woods are another good place to hunt. You should look there after rain in August and also through to October.

If you find a fungus growing on a dead log, check in the **Parasites & Wood-rotters** section. You might find species from the **Mixed Wood** section as well. The picture shows sixteen fungi from this book; how many can you identify?

Amanita muscaria, Boletus appendiculatus, Boletus satanus, Clavariadelphus pistillaris, Coprinus picaceus, Cystolepiota bucknallii, Fistulina hepatica, Geastrum triplex, Lactarius quietus, Laetiporus sulphureus, Leccinum crocipodium, Leccinum versipelle, Mycena pura, Phallus impudicus, Russula mairei, Scleroderma citrinum.

Deciduous Woods

Cystolepiota bucknallii

Do not touch this mushroom. It has a lavender flush down at the base of the stem. The remainder of it is white and the cap surface is powdery. It is very small and is quite common in shady woods and thickets under deciduous trees. It favours rich soils.

Lepiota family
Cap size: 1–2.5 cm – Spore print colour: White
Smell: Coal-gas, unpleasant – Season: Autumn
POISONOUS

Amanita phalloides

Commonly known as the Death Cap, this fungus contains complex chemicals which severely damage the liver and are deadly poisonous. Do not touch it. The cap is yellowish-green to olive, but may also be brownish or even completely white in some forms. The white ring and large bulbous volva are distinctive. Also it has a sweet sickly odour which develops with age and is rather like old honey. It grows, especially in the south, under oaks and occasionally conifers. A white form can be mistaken for a Horse Mushroom (*Agaricus arvensis*, see page 55) but the Horse Mushroom has bright pink gills turning to deep brown, whereas the Death Cap has white gills.

Amanita family
Cap size: 5–15 cm – Spore print colour: White
Smell: With age develops a sickly-sweet odour rather like old honey
Season: Late summer onwards
POISONOUS

Inocybe bongardii

Be careful to identify this poisonous species correctly. It has a pale cinnamon to pinkish-buff cap with darker and flattened scales. The crowded gills are pale brown. It has a silky, fibrous stem. If scratched, the stem stains dull red. Both gills and flesh have a strong, sweet to unpleasant smell of ripe pears. It is fairly common and seems to like heavy clay soils under deciduous trees.

Cortinarius family
Cap size: 2.5-6 cm
Spore print colour: Dull brown
Smell: Sweet to unpleasant ripe pears
Season: Autumn
POISONOUS

Laccaria amethystea

Commonly known as the Amethyst Deceiver. This is one of the most beautiful of all fungi for you to find. You will need to search in the shadier, moister parts of a deciduous woodland. The deep amethyst-violet cap and gills should help you name this species. It changes colour as it dries out to a dull greyish-lilac, although the gills remain violet. A number of fungi change colour on drying and are referred to as 'hygrophanous'.

Tricholoma family
Cap size: 2.5–5 cm
Spore print colour: White
Smell: Not distinctive
Season: Late summer to early winter

Lactarius glyciosmus

As you begin to discover more and more new species you will still be surprised at the odours of some mushrooms. This species for instance has a very strong smell of dried coconut. That smell together with the overall pale greyish-lavender colours make it easy to recognize. When cut it oozes a sticky white latex which is unchanging in colour. Search for it in mixed woodlands.

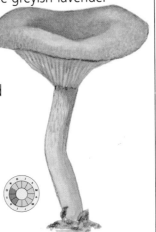

Russula family
Cap size: 2.5–8 cm
Spore print colour: Cream
Smell: Strong of dried coconut
Season: August to autumn

Russula aeruginea

The Russula family has a number of green species. You can help yourself sort them out by the colour of their spores and other features of the cap. This species for instance has deep cream spores and the cap varies from grass-green to yellow-green, often with slight rusty spotting. Some other green species such as *Russula virescens* (see page 38) and *Russula cyanoxantha* (page 14) have white spores. This is a common species you should look for in mixed deciduous woodland.

Russula family
Cap size: 5–10 cm
Spore print colour: Deep cream (D-E)
Smell: None noticeable
Season: Summer and autumn

Clitocybe nebularis

Its common name, Clouded Agaric, refers to the colour of the cap which is a smoky grey-brown. The large smooth cap has a central dome or boss. It grows late in the year, quite often during the first frosts. Sometimes it appears in large fairy rings. You should look for it in deep leaf litter in deciduous woodland. Occasionally it appears in gardens.

Tricholoma family
Cap size: 5-15 cm – Spore print colour: Pale buff
Smell: None – Season: Autumn and early winter

Morchella esculenta

Commonly known as the Yellow or Common Morel. Part of the attraction in hunting for these fungi is the challenge of finding them. You will need all your skill because they fruit for only a short time in the spring. To make your hunt even more difficult they are very fussy about where they will fruit. So begin your search around dying apple trees, elms and ash on chalky soils. The entire mushroom is hollow if cut in half. In an ideal habitat it grows in enormous numbers.

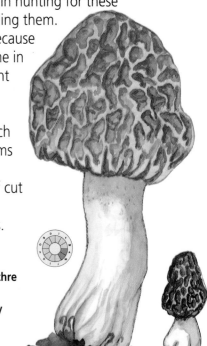

Morel family
Fruit body size: 5–12 cm
Spore print colour: Deep yellow ochre
Smell: Pleasant
Season: End of April to end of May

Deciduous Woods

Lactarius piperatus

This mushroom is white and slightly velvety and soon becomes funnel-shaped. You can check the species by examining the gills, which are so narrow and closely packed that the undersurface of the cap seems to be almost smooth. Like other *Lactarius* species, this one oozes copious latex and in some forms this dries an olive-green. It prefers chalky soils where it is often found under deciduous trees.

Russula family
Cap size: 5–15 cm – Spore print colour: White
Smell: None – Season: August to autumn

Clitocybe geotropa

This can be a very large and upstanding mushroom. Its cap is funnel-shaped and usually with a central umbo. Its colour ranges from white to ivory or pale buff and the surface of the cap is finely roughened.

The margin of the cap is curved in. It often grows in small troops under deciduous trees and seems to prefer chalky soils.

Tricholoma family
Cap size: 5–20 cm
Spore print colour: White
Smell: None or not distinct
Season: Autumn

Marasmius rotula

You will find some mushrooms that are quite tiny. But if you take a very close look you will discover how beautifully they are shaped. This species is a very pretty one with a white bell-shaped cap which is pleated and sunk at the centre. The gills are attached to the stem by a tiny 'collar'. The cap has been likened to an open parachute and that is a good description. Common on dead wood and twigs of deciduous trees.

Tricholoma family
Cap size: 0.15–1 cm – Spore print colour: White
Smell: None noticeable
Season: From early summer continues throughout winter

Pholiota squarrosa

Commonly known as the Shaggy Pholiota. You will recognize this species by the scales that stick out from the cap and stem and its tawny- yellow to russet colour. The gills are crowded, at first yellow then slightly olive, then rust-brown. Be careful if you handle it as there is doubt as to whether it is poisonous or not. Some people may be allergic to it, so leave well alone. You will see it in deciduous woodland at the base of trees or growing out of stumps.

Stropharia family
Cap size: 5–15 cm
Spore print colour: Ochre-brown
Smell: Pungent smell
Season: Autumn
POSSIBLY POISONOUS ☠

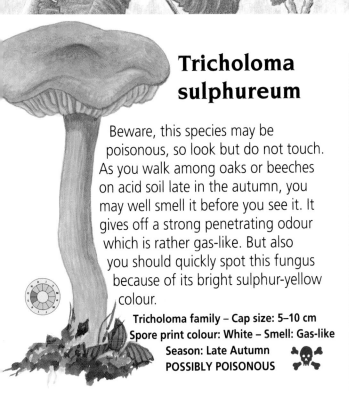

Tricholoma sulphureum

Beware, this species may be poisonous, so look but do not touch. As you walk among oaks or beeches on acid soil late in the autumn, you may well smell it before you see it. It gives off a strong penetrating odour which is rather gas-like. But also you should quickly spot this fungus because of its bright sulphur-yellow colour.

Tricholoma family – Cap size: 5–10 cm
Spore print colour: White – Smell: Gas-like
Season: Late Autumn
POSSIBLY POISONOUS

Boletus subtomentosus

The velvety cap is olive-yellow to rich yellow but it becomes smoother and more reddish brown with age. These colour changes in fungi can make identifying them confusing, but the more often you refer to this book, the easier it will become. Tubes and pores of the *Boletus subtomentosus* are bright yellow and do not turn blue when bruised. It has a narrow and tapering stem often with some coarse ridges or furrows. The flesh is white. It is found in deciduous woods.

Bolete family – Cap size: 5–10 cm
Spore print colour: Olive-brown – Smell: Not distinctive
Season: Summer and autumn

Scleroderma citrinum

Known as the Common Earthball. The Earthballs resemble Puffballs in some respects (see page 7), but their outer wall is tough, leathery and often warty. This species is one of the most abundant in summer and autumn. You will find it everywhere in mixed deciduous woods. It has a very strong, pungent odour, rather like rubber. Its spores are liberated when the upper part breaks open. As you can see in the picture, it is shaped rather like a bun.

Earthball family – Fruit body size: 5–10 cm
Spore print colour: Purple-black – Smell: Rubbery
Season: Summer and autumn – SLIGHTLY POISONOUS

Boletus luridus

This one is perhaps the commonest of a group of species which all have red pores. You should look for it under beech and oak on calcareous soil, particularly in the south. You will see a red network on the stem which turns blue when cut. The matt cap varies from pale orange-ochre to yellow buff and with age to olive. Beware, as it is possibly poisonous, so admire its beauty but do not touch.

Bolete family
Cap size: 7.5–12.5 cm
Spore print colour: Olive-brown
Smell: Not distinctive
Season: Late summer to autumn
POSSIBLY POISONOUS

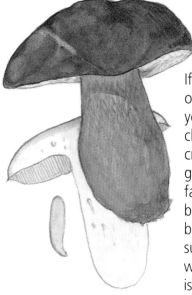

Boletus aereus

If you would like to find a species of record size, this one could be your prize. It has a wonderful chocolate-brown cap which often cracks into a fine mosaic. If it grows up through leaves or some fall on it, this cap becomes blotched with paler patches. The best time to search for it is when summer changes to autumn. You will find it growing under oaks. It is more common in the south of England.

Bolete family
Cap size: 7.5–20 cm – Spore print colour: Olive-brown
Smell: Damp soil, earthy – Season: Late summer and autumn

Boletus appendiculatus

You should look in deciduous woods for this species, especially in central and southern England. Like many fungi, it shows a habitat preference for certain species of tree, in this case oak and beech. Beneath the cap, the tubes and pores are bright yellow, but bruise deep blue when touched. The upper half of the stem shows a yellowish network and its lower half is often flushed reddish-brown.

Bolete family
Cap size: 10–20 cm
Spore print colour: Olive-brown
Smell: Strong rank odour when mature
Season: Summer and autumn

Lactarius quietus

Commonly known as the Oak Milk-cap. If you walk through almost any oak wood in Britain you are almost certain to find this species. *Lactarius quietus* grows only under oaks. Is odour will provide a good clue, too, as it has a sweet, distinctly oily smell. Older mushroom books describe the smell as 'like bed-bugs'! Its latex is yellowish-cream.

Russula family
Cap size: 5–10 cm – Spore print colour: Cream
Smell: Distinctly oily (like some machine oils)
Season: Autumn

Russula atropurpurea

This fungus is very common in mixed woods, especially under oak trees. It has a rich purple-red cap which may be almost black at the centre, and cream gills that are often spotted rust-red. Its name, which was previously used for a different mushroom, is now likely to be changed. Its new name may be *Russula vinacea burlingham*, a species from America which is identical to this one. New information about fungi is constantly being added to what is already known.

Russula family
Cap size: 5–10 cm
Spore print colour: White (A)
Smell: Possibly fruity
Season: Summer and autumn

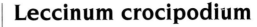

Russula laurocerasi

Fungi often have extraordinary odours, and this is one of the strangest. It has a wonderful smell of bitter almonds or marzipan, but as it ages a sour smell becomes more obvious. The pale honey-brown cap is often very sticky, coarsely ridged and pimpled at the margin. Search for it under oak trees.

Russula family
Cap size: 5–10 cm – Spore print colour: Cream (B-C)
Smell: Bitter almonds. Sour smell on ageing
Season: August to late autumn

Boletus rubellus

You may came upon this species as you walk along a woodland path. Suddenly, under an oak tree, you will see a cluster of bright scarlet or blood-red caps nestled deep in the grass. Both cap and stem bruise blue when handled. It is always to be found close to oak trees, out near the root tips, soon after the first of the late summer rains. Insects find it very attractive.

Bolete family
Cap size: 2–5 cm
Spore print colour: Brown
Smell: None
Season: Late summer to autumn

Leccinum crocipodium

The mosaic of cracks on the cap of this mushroom start yellow but change to dull olive-brown. The surface is often irregular and lumpy. Its pores are bright yellow and bruise brownish. You should search for this species under oak trees. Look for it in those years that are warm and wet, especially in southern England. Its flesh colour changes with age from yellow, then grey-purple, to chestnut and finally blackish. Experience will help you make the necessary age judgement.

Bolete family – Cap size: 5–10 cm
Spore print colour: Olive-brown
Smell: Not distinctive – Season: August to autumn

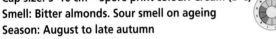

Boletus satanus

Commonly known as Satan's Bolete. A mycologist who described this species said that its smell was so unpleasant that he felt ill even at a distance. It is an uncommon species found under beech and oak on chalky soils in central and southern England. Do not touch this species as it is poisonous.

Bolete family
Cap size: 7.5–30 cm
Spore print colour: Olive-brown
Smell: Foul stench when old
Season: Summer and autumn
POISONOUS

Deciduous Woods

Leccinum scabrum

The dull brown to buff cap of this species provides two clues for you to identify it. Firstly, the cap is soft and if you press it with your finger it usually leaves a depression. Secondly, the species becomes quite sticky in wet weather. Sometimes you may find bright blue-green stains at the base of the stem. The stem has small, darker brown and woolly scales on it. The flesh hardly changes colour when cut. This species grows with birch trees in woods and heaths.

Bolete family
Cap size: 5–15 cm – Spore print colour: Brown
Smell: Pleasant – Season: Summer and autumn

Leccinum variicolor

You should certainly spot this one if it is growing under birch. Its colourful cap is often mottled and oddly blotched, bluish-grey, grey-brown to almost black with white discoloured areas. The pores bruise rose-pink. The stem has dark grey-brown scales and the flesh turns bright rose-pink to reddish-salmon when cut. Add to this the bright blue-green stem base and you have a rainbow of colours.

Bolete family
Cap size: 5–10 cm
Spore print colour: Brown
Smell: Pleasant
Season: Summer and autumn

Lactarius torminosus

Commonly known as the Woolly Milk-cap, this mushroom is interesting to look at, but do not touch. When young, the pink cap starts off quite rolled. Then as it ages, this edge unrolls and reveals a shagg, hairy fringe all around the cap. The gills are pinkish-white as is the stem. If the flesh has been broken, white latex flows copiously. You may come upon it as you search among birches, where it is very comon.

Russula family
Cap size: 5–10 cm – Spore print colour: Cream
Smell: None – Season: Early autumn – POISONOUS

Paxillus involutus

This is a poisonous species, so make sure you recognize it, then leave it alone. The ochre-brown cap has strongly rolled-in edges. When young the margin is woolly and it can be quite sticky when wet. This soon becomes flattened and grooved. The soft, crowded gills are yellowish and bruise quickly rust-brown. It is often abundant in mixed woods where you may find it growing under birch.

Paxillus family
Cap size: 5–15 cm
Spore print colour: Ochre-brown
Smell: None
Season: Late summer and autumn
POISONOUS

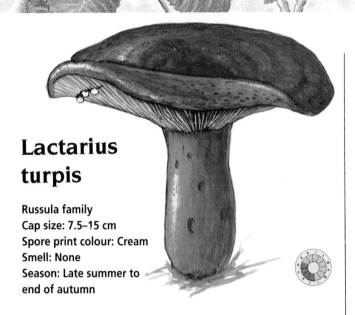

Lactarius turpis

Russula family
Cap size: 7.5–15 cm
Spore print colour: Cream
Smell: None
Season: Late summer to end of autumn

Commonly known as the Ugly Toadstool or Ugly Milk-cap, this mushroom's dark green colour is unusual. The gills are crowded and greenish-white. You will notice that this species gives off a great deal of white latex. You should search around birch trees and even pines, although it is not nearly so common under the latter. It is sticky and slimy to the touch.

Amanita muscaria

Commonly known as Fly Agaric, this poisonous fungus is the traditional fairy-tale toadstool seen in countless children's books. You may find it growing, often in rings, in birch and sometimes pine woods. Its common name refers to its past use in country districts as a remedy against house flies. The skin of the cap was peeled off and placed in a saucer of milk. This attracted flies and the poison quickly killed them. Do not try this yourself. Experimenting with poisonous fungi is dangerous.

Amanita family – Cap size: 7.5–25 cm
Spore print colour: White – Smell: Faint
Season: Late summer and throughout autumn
POISONOUS

Leccinum versipelle

Often referred to as 'Red-Caps' by European collectors, but the cap is not red! It is shades of orange and tawny-yellow, faintly downy and slightly scaly at the centre. The pores are cream, but when bruised turn purple-buff. You will find the stout stem is white or greyish with black-brown scales. The stem base is often flushed green. Use your hand-lens to see the down on the cap and the scales on the stem. This fungus is common among birches.

Bolete family
Cap size: 7.5–20 cm
Spore print colour: Brown-ochre
Smell: None
Season: Summer and autumn

Every fungi expert will tell you that identifying mushrooms and fungi is a tricky business. It takes time to learn how to recognize different species. Many look quite similar to each other and can only be identified under a microscope or by using special chemicals. The best way to identify a fungus is to make a spore print, then look at the spores with your lens.

When you are identifying a fungus, never try to guess what it is. Read as much as you can about the individual species in this book, then try some experiments to see if you can find out more, and ask an expert (see page 78) to help you.

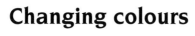

Changing colours

Some mushrooms change colour if they are cut or broken.

1 **Cut the cap and stem** of one or two Bolete mushrooms (see page 6) with a kitchen knife to see if they change colour. Try breaking a piece off the cap with your fingers too.

2 **Press on the cap of a Bolete fungus** with your thumb. Does it turn blue? Why not look through this book and see if you can find out what kind of Bolete it is? (Many Boletes have a name that begins *Boletus*, see the Index.)

3 **Wash your hands afterwards.**

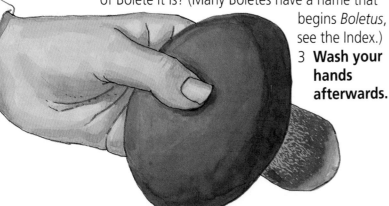

Making a spore print

Every kind of mushroom has different spores, and they can be all sorts of colours. Some mushrooms can only ever be identified by their spores, but every mushroom or fungi in this book has its spore colour detailed in the caption.

It is easy to make your own spore prints, so why not use some of the mushrooms that you find on your expeditions?

1 **Take a sheet of white paper and a sheet of black paper** and overlap them. Fix them together at the back with some sticky tape.

2 **Gently place a small mushroom cap on the joined paper** so that half of it is on one colour and half on the other. Make sure that the underside of the cap is facing down.

3 **Cover the mushroom with a clean, wide-mouthed jar,** and leave it undisturbed for at least 3 hours. Some fungi release their spores very quickly, but others may take up to a day.

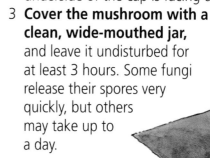

Milk-caps

All 'milk-cap' fungi belong to the *Lactarius* family (see Index for pages where they are shown). They all produce a sticky, milky fluid when they are broken or cut. This fluid is usually white, yellowish, or orange in colour, depending on the species.

If you think you have found a milk-cap fungus, let a drop of the milky fluid fall on to a piece of kitchen paper or a clean paper handkerchief. Wait a few moments to see if it changes colour to green, red, grey, or violet. This will help you to identify which kind of mushroom it is.

Lactarius piperatus

Lactarius Lignyotus

Lactarius Chrysorheus

Fungi smell

Many fungi have a particular sort of smell, which is useful when you are trying to identify a mushroom. Some species smell something like apples, pears, or almonds. Others smell spicy. See how many different smells you can detect and if they remind you of familiar things. Ask others if they agree with you or not. People have different ideas about smells. The most highly-prized edible fungi are the truffles. Some people think they smell delicious, but others don't like the smell at all.

4 **Remove the jar and fungus carefully.** You should see a pattern of either white or coloured specks on the paper. This is the spore print.

5 **Why not add your spore print to your record file** (see page 23)? Spray the print with artist's fixative so that it does not smudge. Buy this from a stationer's or art supplies shop.

6 **Try making decorative spore prints with different kinds of fungi** and see what interesting colours they are.

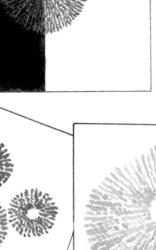

Deciduous Woods

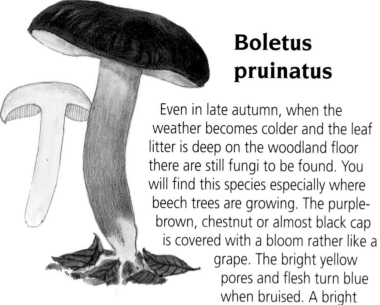

Boletus pruinatus

Even in late autumn, when the weather becomes colder and the leaf litter is deep on the woodland floor there are still fungi to be found. You will find this species especially where beech trees are growing. The purple-brown, chestnut or almost black cap is covered with a bloom rather like a grape. The bright yellow pores and flesh turn blue when bruised. A bright chrome yellow stem completes this rather beautiful member of the Bolete family.

Bolete family
Cap size: 5–10 cm – Spore print colour: Olive-brown
Smell: Not distinct – Season: End of season, late autumn

Geastrum triplex

Commonly known as the Earthstar, it is a most unusual fungus – look for it in beech woods. When young and unopened they look just like a bunch of dark brown onions lying in leaf litter. But the thick leathery outer layer opens up, and a number of fleshy arms curve backwards to reveal the inner ball, surrounded by sort of thick collar. The spores are released by raindrops falling on the ball or by being sucked out by the wind through a tiny hole in the top.

Earthstar family
Fruit body size: 2.5–10 cm
Spore print colour:
Dark brown
Smell: None
Season:
Autumn

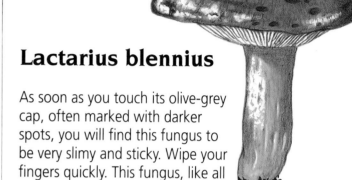

Lactarius blennius

As soon as you touch its olive-grey cap, often marked with darker spots, you will find this fungus to be very slimy and sticky. Wipe your fingers quickly. This fungus, like all *Lactarius* species, releases drops of latex, which in this species is white. It is to be found in beech woods. It can be difficult to identify some fungi, but remember to look carefully before you decide. Think about colour, shape, smell, habitat and other points suggested in this book. Never make a hasty decision.

Russula family
Cap size: 5–10 cm – Spore print colour: Creamy (C)
Smell: Not distinct – Season: Late summer and autumn

Marasmius alliaceus

You should be able to recognize this mushroom by its strong smell of garlic. Notice too, the tall, stiff, black velvety stem and the bell-shaped buff cap. Search for it on fallen beech branches and twigs. Some other *Marasmius* species also smell of garlic but they grow in quite different habitats. *Marasmius scorodonius* grows on needle litter in conifer woods.

Tricholoma family
Cap size: 2.5–5 cm
Spore print colour: Pale cream
Smell: Garlic
Season: Autumn

Micromphale foetidum

This small fungus is a real stinker. It smells of garlic combined with overtones of rotted cabbage or fish. You may find it near beech and hazel. In this habitat it grows in clumps (in contrast to *Marasmius alliaceus*, see opposite) often in large numbers on fallen twigs and branches of those particular trees. The blackish stem is rather short, while the cap is wrinkled, tough and dark brown in colour.

Tricholoma family
Cap size: 1–2.5 cm – Spore print colour: White
Smell: Garlic plus rotted cabbage and fish
Season: Late summer to early autumn

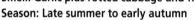

Lepiota aspera

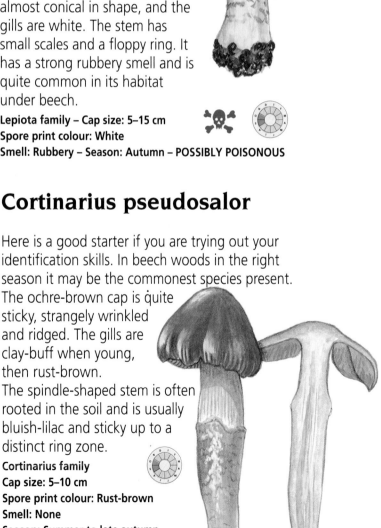

Do not touch this species as it may be poisonous. This species is quite different from most of the Lepiota family, in that the skin of its cap has a powdery or warty surface. In this species, these warts are quite small but sharply pointed. The chestnut cap is almost conical in shape, and the gills are white. The stem has small scales and a floppy ring. It has a strong rubbery smell and is quite common in its habitat under beech.

Lepiota family – Cap size: 5–15 cm
Spore print colour: White
Smell: Rubbery – Season: Autumn – POSSIBLY POISONOUS

Cortinarius armillatus

Here is another easy one to identify. Search for it in beech and birch woods where it sometimes grows in large circles. Look for a fungus with a very bulbous stem with one to three bright red bands of veil circling the stem. The cap is rich brick-red, dry and fibrous. A young one can look very strange. It has a tiny button cap perched upon an enormous rounded bulb.

Cortinarius family
Cap size: 5-10 cm
Spore print colour: Rust-brown
Smell: Not distinct
Season: Late summer to late autumn

Cortinarius pseudosalor

Here is a good starter if you are trying out your identification skills. In beech woods in the right season it may be the commonest species present. The ochre-brown cap is quite sticky, strangely wrinkled and ridged. The gills are clay-buff when young, then rust-brown. The spindle-shaped stem is often rooted in the soil and is usually bluish-lilac and sticky up to a distinct ring zone.

Cortinarius family
Cap size: 5–10 cm
Spore print colour: Rust-brown
Smell: None
Season: Summer to late autumn

Deciduous Woods

Craterellus cornucopiodes

We call this fungus the Horn of Plenty, but the French know it as Trumpet of Death. But it is not poisonous, so the misleading name probably refers to its sombre appearance. You will find the thin, black trumpet is hollow all the way down. It has a brownish and slightly scaly inner surface. This fungus is not easy to find. Look in moist mossy spots such as stream banks, especially where beech grows. It will probably be almost hidden under leaves.

Chanterelle family
Cap size: 2.5–7.5 cm – Spore print colour: White
Smell: Pleasant, fruity – Season: August to late autumn

Russula virescens

Here is a challenge for you. Although this fungus is fairly common and widespread and grows under beech trees, it is particularly attractive to flies. Their larvae enjoy it so much that it is almost impossible to find a complete specimen. If you are fortunate you will enjoy its grey-green, blue-green or yellowish-green cap with its flattened woolly patches. If you find one, there may well be a number growing together.

Russula family
Cap size: 5–10 cm
Spore print colour: White (A)
Smell: Not distinct
Season: Summer and early winter

Cortinarius alboviolaceus

The Latin name *alboviolaceus* means whitish-violet. It is a good description of the overall colours of this species. Its bulbous stem is ringed with a white veil over the lower half. Search for this one in beech woods where it is fairly common. You might confuse it with *Cortinarius argentatus* also found in beech woods, but that one has almost no veil and a distinctly bulbous stem.

Cortinarius family
Cap size: 5 to 10 cm
Spore print colour: Rust-brown
Smell: Faint
Season: Late summer to late autumn

Mycena pura

You may find that the colour of this fungus varies considerably according to habitat. Make a note of which colour you spot in which habitat. The cap varies from a delicate lilac-pink to purplish-grey and even blue-grey. But one thing remains constant: its smell of radishes, which is a common odour in many mushrooms. This species tends to grow under beech among its fallen leaves.

Tricholoma family
Cap size: 2.5–5 cm
Spore print colour: White
Smell: Like radish
Season: Early summer to winter
POSSIBLY POISONOUS

Cortinarius bolaris

This species is now suspected of being dangerously poisonous. It stains with age or handling, the pale yellowish cap and stem become spotted with copper-red scales. It is a fairly common species in beech woods, but you are advised to look and leave alone.

Cortinarius family
Cap size: 5–7.5 cm
Spore print colour: Rust-brown
Smell: Indistinct
Season: Autumn
POISONOUS

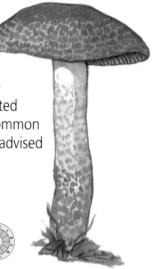

Russula mairei

You might confuse this species with *Russula emetica* (see page 21), as they both have bright red caps. However, *Russula emetica* is found in boggy pine woods, whereas you will find *Russula mairei* in beech woods and never under pine. This is a good example of the value of knowing a species habitat as a help in identification. The gills are white with a faint blue-green hue when young, more cream with age.

Russula family
Cap size: 5–10 cm
Spore print colour: White (A)
Smell: Similar to honey
Season: Late summer and autumn

Mutinus caninus

Although it is a kind of Stinkhorn, this fungus is much less smelly. The slender stem emerges from a small white egg and is white to pale orange. The narrow apex is bright red or orange. Over this apex is spread the dark olive spore mass. You may come across a cluster of *Mutinus caninus* in a beech wood. Like all this family, its colour and smell are aimed at attracting insects. They alight, eat the spores and so later disperse them in their droppings.

Stinkhorn family
Cap size: 7.5–12.5 cm
Spore print colour: Dark olive
Smell: Almost no smell
Season: Late summer to late autumn

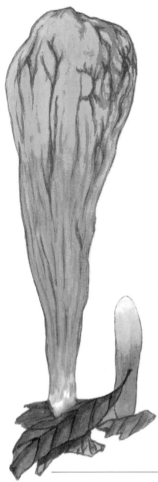

Clavariadelphus pistillaris

Like most people, you will probably be surprised that this is a fungus. It looks rather like a wrinkled club and when young it is quite bright yellow-orange. As it becomes older it turns to ochre-brown or pinkish-brown, often with a lilac tint below. If you cut into the flesh you will see it is white. You may find these fungi in groups standing upright out of the leaf litter in beech woods.

Club Fungi family
Cap size: 7.5–20 cm
Spore print colour: Creamy-white
Smell: Unpleasant
Season: Autumn

Coprinus picaceus

Commonly known as the Magpie Fungus, because of its black and white colours. As it ages the cap slowly dissolves and drips black, inky fluid. The ink of this species along with others, was used in the past as writing ink. Magpie Fungus can be found on beech litter on chalky soils. But you will have to search carefully because it is not common. It is possibly poisonous so is best avoided. Take a good look at the picture and then you will recognize the species in the wood.

Coprinus family
Cap size: 5–10 cm
Spore print colour: Black ☠
Smell: Unpleasant
Season: Late summer to autumn
POSSIBLY POISONOUS

Amanita strobiliformis

This is one of the largest and most striking mushrooms to be found anywhere. Even the young buttons of this species may be larger than the adults of most other species. You should look for this one on chalky soil under beech trees. The entire fungus is pure white and covered with soft, woolly warts or scales. The cap margin is often festooned with ragged veil remnants. You will see a soft ragged ring around the stem.

Amanita family
Cap size: 10–25 cm
Spore print colour: White
Smell: Mild
Season: Mid summer to late autumn

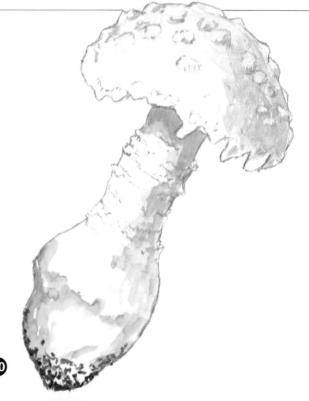

Hydnum repandum

Commonly known as the Hedgehog Mushroom. This is one of the spiny mushroom family. They form their spores on spines or teeth that usually hang down from the underside of the cap. The cap is pale pinkish-orange to orange-buff. Its short spines are pale pinkish-white. The stem is often off-centre. As you walk through a beech wood in autumn you may find a large quantity of them growing in the leaf litter. Sometimes you may see them under conifers and beech.

Toothed Fungi family
Cap size: 5–10 cm
Spore print colour: White
Smell: Pleasant
Season: August to late autumn

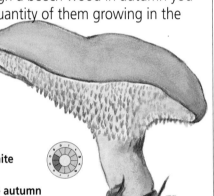

Russula fellea

Commonly known as the Geranium Russula, because of its mild geranium scent. You may well find a large number of them growing together in the deep leaf litter of a beech wood. The whole fungus is honey-yellow or ochre. When damp with rain or dew it is slightly sticky. If you cut it you will find the flesh is white. Although some members of the *Russula* family are difficult to identify, you should have no difficulty with this one.

Russula family
Cap size: 5–10 cm
Spore print colour: Cream (B-C)
Smell: Geranium
Season: Late summer and autumn

Ramaria aurea

The coral-like fruiting body of this magnificent fungus is bright golden-yellow with plenty of tightly packed branches. Each branch ends in a cluster of cauliflower-like tips. The central stem is paler or almost white. It is not a common species, but grows under beech trees.

Ramaria family
Cap size: 5–15 cm
Spore print colour: Deep ochre
Smell: Pleasant
Season: Late summer and autumn

Ramaria botrytis

This is a cauliflower-like species of coral fungi. Its broad central stem is split into numerous smaller branches. Each little branch is tipped with delicate pinkish-purple. Members of the family resemble undersea corals and are among the brightest coloured fungi to be found. This one is a rare species, but if you search in a beech wood in autumn you may find some.

Coral Fungi family
Cap size: 5–15 cm
Spore print colour: Pale ochre
Smell: Fruity
Season: Autumn

How Fungi Spread

Unlike plants, fungi spread by producing microscopic specks, called 'spores', instead of seeds. Each fungus makes billions of spores, which are carried away on the wind, or by animals, to land and grow in a new place.

The most important part of a fungus is the 'mycelium', which is like a meshwork of threads. They can be finer than a hair or as thick as a boot lace. The mycelium is often hidden under tree bark or in the soil. Some kinds of mycelium stretch for many metres underground or inside a tree or rotting log.

The mushroom cap itself is called the 'fruiting body' (see page 6), and its only function is to spread the spores when the climate and other conditions are right. Once the spores have been spread, the fruiting body rots away, or is eaten by slugs and other animals. But the mycelium carries on living, even though you cannot usually see it.

Smelly stinkhorns

You can smell a Stinkhorn fungus (see page 7) long before you see it. If you can bear to stand close to one, you might see lots of flies buzzing around and settling on it. The flies are attracted to the Stinkhorn by its horrible smell, which is like rotting meat. All the insects that land on the fungus will carry some of its spores with them when they fly away, and new Stinkhorns will grow elsewhere.

Puffballs in the rain

If you find some Puffball fungi (see page 7), you can do this simple experiment to see how they release their spores. All you need is a small bottle of tap water or use an eye dropper if you can find one.

1 **Hold the bottle above the Puffball** and drip 4–5 drops of water on to the top of it.
2 **The top of the Puffball will burst open** and a cloud of spores will puff out, if it is ripe and ready to spread its spores.
3 **If this doesn't happen,** look for a riper Puffball.

Mushy mushrooms

The caps of some fungi dissolve as they release their spores. Here is an experiment to do if you can find an Ink Cap (look up *Coprinus* species in the Index).

1 **Look for an Ink Cap mushroom** that has not started to drip its black ink yet.
2 **Carry it home carefully** in a twist of paper (see page 23) or in a plastic or cardboard box.
3 **Take a lump of modelling clay or Blu-tack** and roll it into a sausage shape.
4 **Stand the mushroom upright on an old plate,**

4 **If you see some ripe Puffballs and you don't have any water with you,** try blowing across the top of the Puffball gently, imitating a gust of wind, to see if it puffs out its spores.

5 **Look out for old Puffballs that have already burst** open. They are a completely different colour and soon start rotting away.

then wind the sausage shape around the bottom of the stem to keep it in position.

5 **Wash your hands afterwards.**

6 **After a few days** the Ink Cap will begin to drip ink as it spreads its spores. The cap gradually turns black and eventually it will dissolve away.

Fairy rings

Several kinds of mushrooms, including *Marasmius oreades* (see page 54), and *Calocybe gambosum* (see page 59) grow in a circle. You can often find these circles, known as fairy rings, in meadows, parklands, and on garden lawns.

When you find a fairy ring, compare the colour of the grass inside the ring of mushrooms with the grass on the outside.

The grass on the inside is often poor and there may even be bare patches. The grass on the outside of the ring, especially next to the mushrooms, is often long and very green. This difference in the grass is caused by the mycelium, which grows underground from the centre of the ring outwards, breaking down and using the nutrients in the soil as it spreads. The broken down nutrients fertilize the grass around the edge, making it long and lush.

Bonfire & forest fires

Some fungi only grow where an area has been burned, like the site of a forest fire or a bonfire. If you find an area like this you may be lucky enough to see several kinds of cup fungi. If a forest fire sweeps through an area, there are usually lots of fungi growing there the following year, before all the trees and other plants have grown back.

Conifer Woods

Conifers are evergreen trees with needles instead of leaves. Evergreen trees grow and shed their leaves or needles all the year round. Probably the only place you will find a naturally seeded conifer wood is in Scotland, and they are rare there.

However, there are many conifer plantations all over Great Britain, particularly in East Anglia, Wales and Scotland. Many have been planted by the Forestry Commission (see page 78). The best time to look for fungi in conifer woods is between September and November. Again many fungi only grow in partnership with one type of tree, while certain parasite fungi only grow on pine stumps (see pages 66–77). This picture shows twelve fungi from the next section; how many can you recognize?

Agaricus silvaticus, Auriscalpum vulgare, Cortinarius traganus, Gomphideus roseus, Lactarius deliciosus, Marasmius androsaceus, Morchella elata, Paxillus atrotomentosus, Russula emitica, Suillus grevellei, Suillus luteus, Tricholomopsis rutilans.

Cortinarius traganus

This beautiful fungus is a clear, lilac-lavender with some whitish veil remnants spread over cap and stem. If you cut into it you will find the flesh is a marbled, bright yellow-brown. It is to be found in the pine woods of Scotland. Experts describe its strong pungent odour as over-ripe pears, goats or acetylene gas.

Cortinarius family
Cap size: 5–10 cm – Spore print colour: Rust-brown
Smell: Over-ripe pears, goats or acetylene gas
Season: End of summer and autumn

Russula xerampelina

This mushroom has it all: beautiful colours, strange odour and colour-changing flesh. The cap is deep purple to wine-red, sometimes almost black at the centre. Its surface is dry and slightly wrinkled. The stem is a beautiful purplish-red or pink, but stains yellow-brown when handled. As it ages it smells strongly of old fish or crab. It is rather uncommon, but you should look for it in pine woods.

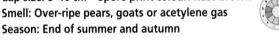
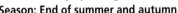

Russula family
Cap size: 5–10 cm
Spore print colour: Pale ochre
Smell: Old fish or crab
Season: Summer and autumn

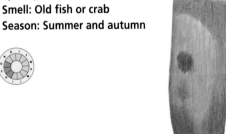

Gomphidius glutinosus

This species is rather uncommon. It grows in groups under conifers especially spruce. You will find it a very slimy mushroom, but it is very attractive. Notice the glutinous ring zone and the bright yellow stem base. While uncommon or rare species may add a challenge to your fungi hunting, a long list of common fungi in your field notebook is even more of a prize.

Gomphidius family
Cap size: 5–10 cm – Spore print colour: Black
Smell: Not distinctive – Season: Late summer to autumn

Tricholomopsis rutilans

Commonly known as Plums and Custard, because of its purplish-yellow cap colour. It is really a combination of tiny wine-red scales on the yellow background. The gills are bright golden-yellow. This species is a good example of why you should never judge spore colour by the colour of the gills, as it has golden gills, but white spores. Look for it on or near conifer stumps or in the sawdust left by felling the trees.

Tricholoma family
Cap size: 5–15 cm
Spore print colour: White
Smell : Wet, rotten wood
Season: End of summer to late autumn

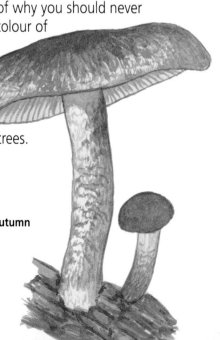

Conifer Woods

Auriscalpium vulgare

Commonly known as the Earpick Fungus. The name *auriscalpium* is Latin for 'earpick' and refers to a small instrument used by the Romans for personal hygiene. It resembled this fungus in shape. The spoon-shaped, scaly and dark brown cap has tiny spines on its underside. It is particularly interesting because it grows only on fallen and partly rotted pine cones. Search for it carefully in the cool and shady pine woods because it is small and easily overlooked.

Toothed Fungi family
Cap size: 1–2.5 cm – Spore print colour: White
Smell: None easy to detect – Season: All year

Suillus luteus

The common name, Slippery Jack, refers to the cap, which is damp and sticky in wet weather. You will find this species among the needles under pine trees. Under the cap, the tubes are lemon-yellow to straw colour and the pores a similar colour. In its early stage it is covered by a thin veil. You will easily recognize the stem which is covered with glandular dots at the top. It has a thin white ring, usually flushed violet on the underside.

Bolete family
Cap size: 5–10 cm
Spore print colour: Olive-brown
Smell: Not distinctive
Season: Late summer into autumn

Marasmius androsaceus

The common name, Horsehair Fungus, refers to the very thin, hair-like, blackish-brown stems of this species. They are very long and the tiny (often less than 1 cm), fluted, brown caps are balanced on top. The few gills are fluted brown and widely spaced. If you explore a conifer wood, search among the fallen cones and needle litter and you may find them growing in very large numbers.

Tricholoma family
Cap size: 0.6–1 cm – Spore print colour: White
Smell: Not distinctive – Season: Late spring to early winter

Agaricus silvaticus

You will find the common name, the Red-staining Mushroom, appropriate. If you find this species and scratch the stem or cap, a bright scarlet stain will appear in a few minutes. Undamaged the cap is light yellow-brown to russet-brown and is covered with fine scales. It has pink gills which go dark brown with age. The stem, which is slightly bulbous and white, is smooth below the fragile ring. This mushroom is common in coniferous woods.

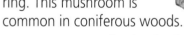

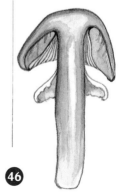

Agaricus family
Cap size: 5–10 cm
Spore print colour: Deep brown
Smell: Not distinctive
Season: Late summer and autumn

Clitocybe clavipes

The Latin for club-foot is *clavipes* and this describes the shape of the grey-brown stem as it swells out at the base. Its slightly domed, grey-brown to ochre-brown cap contrasts with the pale yellow-cream gills. You will find it growing in conifer woods, especially those with pine. In dry weather the cap is velvety, but in wet it is very slippery to the touch.

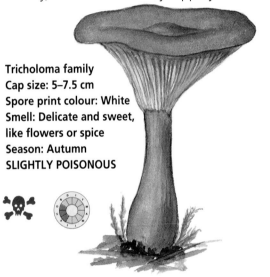

Tricholoma family
Cap size: 5–7.5 cm
Spore print colour: White
Smell: Delicate and sweet, like flowers or spice
Season: Autumn
SLIGHTLY POISONOUS

Gomphidius roseus

This is an extraordinarily beautiful species. You will find it among the dark needle litter with its sticky, bright coral-pink cap shining under the shade of the pines. There is a mystery attached to this fungus. Wherever it grows, it is found close to *Suillus bovinus* (a pink to brown capped Bolete). Why is a mystery, but it seems the fruiting of one is stimulated by the other.

Gomphidius family
Cap size: 2.5–5 cm
Spore print colour: Almost black
Smell: Not noticeable
Season: Late summer and autumn

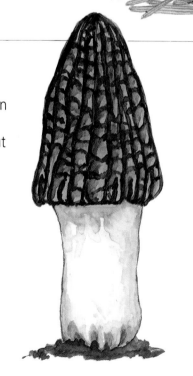

Morchella elata

Commonly known as the Black Morel. There remain many facts to be discovered about this species. Experts have many different ideas about sorting out and classifying the various species of morels. Here is a chance for you to help discover more details as to its habitat preferences. Does it prefer conifers to ash trees? It grows only in the spring, so this is one of the first species to search for in the new year.

Cup Fungi family
Fruit body size: 5–12.5 cm
Spore print colour: Pale ochre
Smell: Pleasant
Season: Springtime

Conifer Woods

Lycoperdon pyriforme

When you find some of these, tap them lightly and you may see the spores puff out, (see also Activity on page 42). Search for them on old pine stumps in conifer woods, where they often grow in large clusters. Rather pear-shaped, they are white when young, but turn brownish-grey with age. If you find some that appear to be growing in soil, gently scrape at the soil and you will find them attached to either a dead and buried branch or rotting root.

Puffball family
Fruit body size: 2–4.5 cm – Spore print colour: Olive-brown
Smell: Slightly fishy – Season: Summer and autumn

Suillus granulatus

The genus *Suillus* can be recognized by the small glandular dots on the upper part of the stem, the often sticky cap (although some are dry and scaly) and their strict relationship to one species of conifer. This species has all these features. It is found under pine often in large numbers. It often weeps latex when young. If you cut the flesh you will see it is pale yellow and it does not change colour on exposure to the air.

Bolete family
Cap size: 5–10 cm
Spore print colour: Yellowish-brown
Smell: Pleasant
Season: Late summer and autumn

Tricholoma terreum

There are a number of grey *Tricholoma* species, not all easy to name. You will need to check very closely, texture of cap surface and colour of gill edges. In this species you should look for a finely velvety grey to grey-brown cap. The gills are broad, grey-white and notched where they join the stem. You may find them under pines where they often grow in large numbers.

Tricholoma family
Cap size: 5–10 cm
Spore print colour: White
Smell: Almost odourless
Season: Late summer to late autumn

Mycena epipterygia

You should be able to find this species because it is common in mossy areas under conifers. The best habitat to search is under both conifers and bracken on heaths and moors as well as on dead conifer wood. If you touch it you will find both cap and stem are very sticky, especially in wet weather. Its cap is found in many variations of pale greenish-yellow, becoming greyer with age.

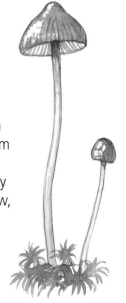

Tricholoma family
Cap size: 0.6–1 cm
Spore print colour: White
Smell: Not distinctive
Season: Autumn

Suillus grevillei

Here is a mushroom that you will only find near larch trees. It often forms a circle around these trees. Look for its bright yellow-orange cap and stem. The yellow pores bruise reddish-brown. The stem has a white, cottony ring at the top. As you grow more familiar with fungi you will find this one to be the commonest species of *Suillus*. If you are in Scotland you may find a deep reddish-chestnut variety, but the rest of its details are identical.

Bolete family
Cap size: 5–15 cm
Spore print colour: Yellowish
Smell: Not distinctive
Season: Late summer to autumn

Chroogomphus rutilus

The often large cap of this species frequently has a sharp dome in the middle. The cap is sticky when wet, but it dries quickly and is orange-brown to copper-red and shiny. The gills start off as an ochre colour, but turn to purplish-grey when mature. It is a common species and one you should hunt for under pine trees and among the needles. The solid flesh is ochre-orange.

Gomphidius family
Cap size: 5–15 cm
Spore print colour: Blackish
Smell: Pleasant
Season: Autumn

Lactarius deliciosus

Commonly known as the Saffron Milk Cap. This bright species is to be found, often in large numbers, under pine. The cap is bright orange with salmon coloured blotches in concentric circles. As it ages the cap stains or discolours slightly green. If you accidentally damage the gills or flesh they ooze an orange milk. The stem is orange and frequently has small round pits or spots.

Russula family
Cap size: 5–10 cm
Spore print colour: Cream
Smell: Not distinct
Season: late summer and autumn

A Close Look At Fungi

There are lots of interesting fungi experiments that you can do at home. If you look at mushrooms more closely, you can see what they look like inside and how some change colour and shape. When you collect fungi for experiments, never pick poisonous ones (see page 5).

If possible, put your collection of fungi in the fridge as soon as you get home. This will keep them fresh until you start your experiments.

Hatching fungi 'eggs'

Stinkhorns (see page 7) develop inside egg-shaped fruit bodies. If you find one of these, take it home to see if you can hatch it.

1 **Place the fungus on some damp tissue paper** inside a plastic container with a lid and leave it for a day or two. The Stinkhorn really does stink once it has hatched, so keep the lid on the container and put it outside or in a shed.

2 **Wash your hands afterwards.**

3 **The Stinkhorn egg will probably hatch during the night** or early in the morning. It's a good idea to hold your nose when you take the lid off the container.

4 **If you find more than one** Stinkhorn egg to experiment with, cut one in half to see how the Stinkhorn fungus has begun to form inside.

Watch mushrooms grow

See if you can make a mushroom continue to grow once it has been picked. You will need a young button mushroom for this experiment.

1 **Take a young button mushroom,** either a wild species or one that you have bought from a shop and measure the cap and the stem, making a note of the size.

2 **Place the mushroom in a jar** on a piece of damp kitchen paper.

3 **Check the mushroom once a day** over the next two or three days to see if it has grown in size. If it seems larger, measure it again.

4 **Make a note of any changes** in your field notebook (see page 22):
- How much has it increased in size?
- Has the cap opened to reveal the gills underneath?
- Look closely at the gills. Have they changed colour as the mushroom matures?

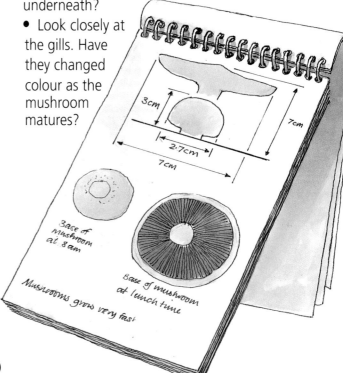

3cm

2.7cm

7cm

7cm

Base of mushroom at 8am

Base of mushroom at lunch time

Mushrooms grow very fast

Mobile mushrooms

1 **Lay the mushroom on its side** on a plate and leave it on a table for several hours.
2 **When you return** you will see that the stem of the mushroom has bent so that the cap is lying parallel to the table top.
3 **Try this experiment with other kinds of fungi.** Does the same thing happen?

Some mushrooms always turn their caps so that they are level with the ground. This may be because it is easier for the spores to fall out when the cap is horizontal. Look for a non-poisonous *Amanita* (like *Amanita citrina*, see page 18) and take it home.

Spongy fungi

Some kinds of fungi, such as the Boletes (see page 6) have spongy pores on the underside of their caps instead of gills. Compare this kind of mushroom with one that has gills.

1 **On a rainy day, pick a Bolete** so that you can look at the pores more closely. Press the cap with your thumb and see how water oozes out, rather like a bath sponge.

2 **If you have a magnifying glass,** look at the cap through it. You can see that the spongy part is made up of masses of tiny tubes. These tubes contain the spores.

3 **Try cutting the cap in half**, or see if you can peel the layer of sponge away from the rest of the cap to see the tubes more closely.

The Artist's Fungus

If you are lucky enough to find an Artist's Fungus (*Ganoderma applanatum*, see page 67) on one of your mushroom hunts, take it home to discover why it has this unusual name.

1 **Using a sharp stick, scratch a simple drawing** into the underside of the fungus. Your design will gradually change colour like magic.
2 **If you leave the fungus to dry out** for a week or two, your picture will be permanent and you can add it to your fungus collection.
3 **If you visit a museum with a collection of fungi,** you may see drawings done by other people. Some of these are hundreds of years old.

Open Spaces

This habitat includes gardens, parks, fields, pastures, roadsides, hedgerows and open ground everywhere. In the summer they tend to be rather dry, but after rain in late summer and the autumn they often produce species that you will not find anywhere else.

Often these sites have been grazed or trampled by animals, so you may find fungi growing from the droppings that they have left. Check carefully to see if the fungus is growing from animal dung. If it is, and you take a specimen, be sure to wash your hands carefully afterwards.

Hedgerows are worth checking for fungi from the **Parasites** section as well. Did you know that, as a general rule, a hedgerow gains one species of tree for every hundred years that it has existed? The more species of tree you find, the older the hedge you are searching is likely to be. If you are searching a hedgerow beside a road, or checking verges, try to go with a friend. Then one of you can watch for traffic and the other can hunt for fungi.

You are very likely to find fairy rings (see page 43) in this habitat, although not along roads or in hedgerows. You should also check bonfire sites in gardens and parks for the particular fungi that grow on burnt ground (see page 43 again). This picture shows thirteen fungi from the next section; see how many you can identify.

Agaricus arvensis, Agarius bitorquis, Aleuria aurantia, Coprinus comatus, Hygrocybe conica, Hygrocybe punicea, Langermannia gigantea, Lycoperdon perlatum, Macrolepiota procera, Marasmius oreades, Panaeolus sphinctrinus, Psathyrella velutina, Stropharia semiglobata.

Open Spaces

Hygrocybe psittacina

This species well deserves its common name, the Parrot Mushroom. It is one of the few truly green mushrooms, and, like a parrot, it can be a mixture of different shades mixed with yellow and orange. These colours fade as it ages. The smooth cap is very slippery to the touch when wet. The gills often have a notch where they join the stem. (Compare with *Hygrocybe laeta*, page 57.) Look for it late in the season in grassy woodlands, fields and pastures everywhere.

Hygrophorus family
Cap size: 1. 5–2.5 cm
Spore print colour: White
Smell: Not distinctive
Season: Summer to early winter

Macrolepiota procera

Commonly known as the Parasol Mushroom. One day you may be really fortunate and discover a group of these magnificent Parasols growing out of the grass in a field. They have been found up to 45 cm tall. In older specimens you can slide the whitish double-layered ring up and down the stem. Can you see how it got its name?

Lepiota family
Cap size: 10–25 cm average
Spore print colour: White to cream
Smell: Indistinct
Season: Late summer to autumn

Entoloma incanum

The most curious and pungent smell of this species may help you identify it. Experts describe the smell as being like mice or burnt hair. The stem is bright olive-green to blue-green. The cap is olive-green, then brownish, with fine lines and the centre is depressed. It is quite common in open pastureland on chalky soils.

Entoloma family
Cap size: 2–2.5 cm
Spore print colour: Pink
Smell: Mice or burnt hair
Season: Late summer and autumn

Marasmius oreades

Commonly known as the Fairy Ring Mushroom. Although many other species of fungi form fairy rings this is the most well-known. You will find the large rings of dark green grass on lawns, golf courses and playing fields. On their outer edge you will see these mushrooms. The rings grow larger each year and some are known that are many hundreds of metres across. Those are thought to be over a thousand years old. It has been suggested that some rings may be among the oldest inhabitants of this planet. Be very careful not to confuse this species with the dangerously poisonous, white capped *Clitocybe rivulosa*. You may well find them growing together.

Tricholoma family
Cap size: 2.5–7.5 cm
Spore print colour: White
Smell: Faint, but of fresh sawdust
Season: Summer and autumn

Hygrocybe conica

This fungus is attractive and you should be able to find it in fields and grassy woodlands everywhere. Look at the shape of the bright red cap and the yellowish, flushed red slender stem. The gills are yellowish. If you bruise it anywhere all parts turn black and within a few hours the entire mushroom will look completely blackened – a very quick and easy-to-recognize colour change.

Hygrophorus family
Cap size: 2.5–5 cm – Spore print colour: White
Smell: Not distinctive – Season: Mid-summer and autumn

Agaricus campestris

Commonly known as the Field Mushroom, Pink-bottom, or Champignon, this is similar to the mushroom you buy in your local shop. It grows in large fairy rings. However, if you see it in its open grass habitat be careful not to confuse it with *Agaricus xanthodermus* (page 59). The Field Mushroom flushes slightly reddish-pink to brown if you cut it. The poisonous *Agaricus xanthodermus* goes bright yellow.

Agaricus family – Cap size: 5–10 cm
Spore print colour: Deep brown
Smell: Pleasant, almonds – Season: June-October

Hygrocybe punicea

This is a magnificent species, but sadly rather rare. Its bright scarlet to blood-red cap and stem will feel silky or greasy. The gills are thick and waxy, and are coloured yellowish to orange. A key characteristic of this species is that both the flesh and the base of the stem are whitish. This species is well worth looking for, so search carefully in the fields and pastures which are its habitat.

Hygrophorus family
Cap size: 5–10 cm
Spore print colour: White
Smell: Not distinctive
Season: Autumn

Agaricus arvensis

Commonly known as the Horse Mushroom. You should search for this species in fields and woodland clearings. It has a white, smooth to scaly cap which ages brassy yellow. Its gills are pale pink, then deep brown. The club-shaped stem is white with a slightly woolly surface below the ring. The flesh is white and bruises slight ochre. It smells slightly of aniseed. But take care! If brilliant yellow stains develop and it smells unpleasantly iodine-like, turn to page 59 and read the description of the similar but poisonous *Agaricus xanthodermus*.

Agaricus family
Cap size: 10–15 cm
Spore print colour: Deep brown
Smell: Aniseed
Season: Late summer and autumn

Open Spaces

Panaeolus sphinctrinus

This is a species that grows in grass, often on animal dung. The silvery-grey cap is bell-shaped. When young it has tiny white 'teeth' around the cap's margin. These are remnants of the veil. The gills are greyish and, like all *Panaeolus* species, become mottled with black as the spores mature. It seems to prefer horse or cow dung. Pastures and fields are good places to search.

Coprinus family
Cap size: 2.5–5 cm
Spore print colour: Blackish
Smell: Not distinctive
Season: Late spring into summer and autumn

Fairy Rings

In folklore there are many explanations for fairy rings. For instance, they are said to be caused by fairies dancing, lightning striking, animals running in circles or witches cauldrons. There is one rather macabre explanation which says they are caused by a buried body. In reality, they are the natural result of the steady outward growth and expansion of the fungus's mycelium. It radiates out in this circular fashion and fruits on the actively-growing outside edge.

Clavulinopsis fusiformis

You should be able to find this club fungus in grasslands and open woods everywhere. The simple, narrow clubs are pointed at the tips and are loosely clustered. They have hollow centres and are very brittle. Look closely and you will see the clubs are not truly fused together at a common base, but are separate, unlike some other yellow club fungi.

Club Fungi family
Cap size: 5–15 cm – Spore print colour: Cream
Smell: Not distinctive – Season: Autumn

Bovista plumbea

Here is a Puffball fungus which looks like a small golf ball when young. As it grows older, the outer white skin flakes away to expose a lead-grey inner surface. The olive-brown spore mass is enclosed within. You may came across it in pastures and lawns providing the grass is short. Try tapping it gently and, if it is ripe, it will puff out its dry powdery spores.

Puffball family
Fruit body size: 2–3 cm
Spore print colour: Olive. Puff some on to your paper
Smell: Indistinct
Season: Late summer and autumn

Stropharia semiglobata

Its common name, Dung Roundhead, is a good description of both its preferred habitat and its appearance. You may see this fungus as you walk through fields where sheep, cattle and horses have been kept. It grows on their dung. The small cap is sticky when wet, and a pale to bright yellow-ochre. The gills are a pale lilac-brown. The stem is sticky below the narrow ring.

Stropharia family
Cap size: 2.5–5 cm
Spore print colour: Purple-brown
Smell: Not distinctive
Season: Spring, summer and autumn

Hygrocybe laeta

You could confuse this species with *Hygrocybe psittacina* (see page 54) but there are some clear differences. The green tints in this species are confined to the gills and the top of the stem. The cap is in shades of orange to olive-brown or orange-brown and is slimy when wet. The gills vary from white to olive to greyish-pink. You may find it growing in pastures, fields and moors often among bracken.

Hygrophorus family
Cap size: 1–2.5 cm
Spore print colour: White
Smell: Not distinctive
Season: Autumn

Bolbitius vitellinus

Some fungi, including this one, tend to break up very easily. The beautiful yellow cap is sticky and has deep grooves when old. If you examine the stem with your hand lens, you will see it has a hairy surface. As it becomes older, this fungus collapses and it rarely lasts more than a few hours. Look for it on rotted straw, dung and manured grassland.

Bolbitius family
Cap size: 2–5 cm – Spore print colour: Rust-ochre
Smell: Not distinctive – Season: Summer and autumn

Volvariella speciosa

To find this species you should explore old grass in fields, straw heaps or around stables and dung heaps. Its silky white-grey cap is often sticky. The broad gills are completely free of the stem, white and then deep pink. The tall stem emerges from a small thick volval cup usually buried in the grass. The spores are deep salmon-pink. Be very careful not to confuse this fungus with a poisonous *Amanita*. All this family have volvas, but always have white spores, never pink.

Pluteus family
Cap size: 5–10 cm
Spore print colour: Pink. Check this colour carefully
Smell: Mild and earthy
Season: Mid summer and autumn

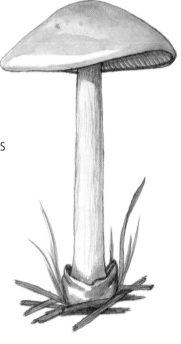

Open Spaces

Leucocoprinus birnbaumi

To find this uncommon species you will have to look indoors! It grows in potted house plants and greenhouses. This fungus is an example of a species imported from the tropics. Its cap is pleated with minute lines. You cannot mistake its brilliant yellow, fragile body if you find one in its warm indoor habitat.

Lepiota family – Cap size: 2–3 cm – Spore print colour: White
Smell: Indistinct – Season: All year

Langermannia gigantea

Commonly known as the Giant Puffball, this is one of the monsters of the fungus world. Giant specimens are said to have been mistaken for resting sheep. Someone once estimated even an average sized one may produce 7,000 billion spores. Despite this, in some years this species is uncommon. If you chance upon a good fruiting year you may find them appearing by the hundred. Search along banks and hedgerows, woodland edges, fields and gardens. This puffball is rather flattened and has a suede-like skin.

Puffball family – Fruit body size: 20–50 cm across
Spore print colour: Yellow-brown
Smell: Indistinct – Season: Summer into autumn

Panaeolus foenisecii

If you have a lawn, the chances are you will one day see this extremely common mushroom growing there. The rounded to flattened cap starts date-brown in colour, but quickly dries to pale pinkish-buff. Look carefully at the gills and you will see they are widely spaced and dark brown. Experts differ as to which genus it belongs. Some say it is a *Panaeolus*, others a *Panaeolina* or even a *Psathyrella*.

Coprinus family
Cap size: 1–2.5 cm – Spore print colour: Purple-brown
Smell: Indistinct – Season: Late summer and autumn

Clitocybe nuda

Commonly known as the Wood Blewit. This is a common species and you could find it in large numbers, often in rings at the end of the year. You will recognize the deep violet cap, gills and stem. Older specimens have a brownish cap. Its name could mislead you into thinking it is only found in woods, but they are often commonly found on roadsides and in gardens. Be careful not to confuse it with some of the violet-purple *Cortinarius* species.

Tricholoma family
Cap size: 5–15 cm
Spore print colour: Pale pinkish-buff
Smell: Pleasant flowery, fruity
Season: Autumn
to year's end

Lycoperdon perlatum

Commonly known as the Common Puffball. You will find this extremely common species growing in fields, roadsides and gardens, as well as grassy clearings in woods. The ball is very slightly club-shaped. It has small white spines or warts over its surface, often in tiny rings, which you can easily rub off. It starts life snow-white, but soon becomes discoloured brownish. Tap it and you may see the spores puff out through a pore in the top.

Puffball family
Fruit body size: 2.5–5 cm
Spore print colour: Olive-ochre
Smell: Indistinct
Season: Late summer and early autumn

Calocybe gambosum

This mushroom is commonly known as St George's Mushroom, as it appears early in the season, around St George's Day, 26 April. It has a fleshy cap and stem. If you look closely at a specimen you will see the gills are narrow and crowded, usually notched at the stem. It is a species that often grows in fairy rings. For a habitat it prefers grassy woodlands, hedgerows or fields. Some species of *Entoloma* are also to be found in spring, but they have pink spores.

Tricholoma family
Cap size: 5–15 cm
Spore print colour: Cream
Smell: Meal or cucumber
Season: May and June

Leucoagaricus leucothites

Be careful with your identification of this species. It is all too easy to confuse it with the Field Mushroom (*Agaricus campestris*, see page 55), especially because the gills are pinkish when mature. If you examine a specimen you will find that the gills never darken to blackish-brown as in the Field Mushroom. It has an unusual characteristic – if you take a series of spore prints over a period of time you will discover each print is darker and pinker than the one before. It is found in open fields and on woodland edges.

Lepiota family – Cap size: 5–10 cm
Spore print colour: At first white but later darker and pinker.
Best avoided
Smell: Not distinctive
Season: Autumn

Agaricus xanthodermus

Commonly known as the Yellow Stainer. This is an infamous, poisonous mushroom because it is often confused with either the Field Mushroom (*Agaricus campestris*, see page 55) or the Horse Mushroom (*Agaricus arvensis*, also see page 55). But in the Yellow Stainer the white cap soon ages greyish and becomes fibrous or scaly and the cap or stem when scratched turn a brilliant chrome-yellow. Its flesh smells unpleasantly of iodine and the stem is bulbous with a ring and cottony patches on its underside. It grows in hedges, gardens and rubbish tips.

Agaricus family – Cap size: 7.5–12.5 cm
Spore print colour: Deep brown
Smell: Unpleasantly of iodine or ink
Season: Summer and autumn – POISONOUS

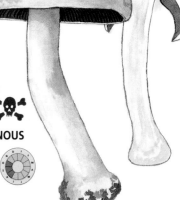

Open Spaces

Lepiota cristata

The common name, Stinking Lepiota, refers to the strong and unpleasant smell of rubber, which is present in the gills and flesh. It has a white cap well-marked with dark reddish-brown scales. The smooth white stem has a tiny white ring near the top. Search for it in grassy areas in mixed woods on roadsides and in gardens, but leave it untouched.

Lepiota family – POSSIBLY POISONOUS
Cap size: 1–5 cm – Spore print colour: White
Smell: Rubbery – Season: Autumn

Lyophyllum decastes

One day you may see an enormous clump of brownish mushrooms that have pushed up through soil, gravel or even tarmac. Indeed this species shows a preference for roadsides and tracks. The caps will feel dry to your touch. The stout, firm, smooth, white stems are often offset from the centre of the cap. It is said that it is often attached to buried roots.

Tricholoma family
Cap size: 5–10 cm
Spore print colour: White
Smell: Indistinct
Season: Summer and autumn

Psathyrella velutina

Commonly known as Weeping Widow. You may have observed how some fungi favour disturbed habitats. This is an example and you will find it along tracks and paths in woodlands, where walking feet cause disturbance. The pale reddish-brown cap is fibrous, often with a ragged margin. The gills are deep yellow, then black with white edges. They often weep drops of moisture, hence the common name. The shaggy stem has a ring-zone at the top.

Coprinus family
Cap size: 2.5–7.5 cm – Spore print colour: Blackish-brown
Smell: Indistinct – Season: Late spring through to autumn

Stropharia aeruginosa

Commonly known as Verdigris Agaric. You could regard this as the model on which all other toadstools are based. It has a slimy cap, and strange poisonous-looking colours. Its appearance is weird with its bright blue-green cap with white flecks of veil at its edge. The gills are deep violet-brown. A greenish stem is clothed in white scales up to a well-formed ring. Search in rich soil, woodland paths or grass at the edge of woodland.

Stropharia family
Cap size: 2.5–7.5 cm
Spore print colour: Violet-brown
Smell: Indistinct
Season: Early summer to late autumn

Agaricus bitorquis

You may be surprised to see how mushrooms often push up through and out of hard soils. You may find this species, more than any other, bursting up through hard-packed soil, tarmac or even concrete. Some have been seen to lift up paving slabs. This strength comes from their ability to take in water as they expand upwards. This species has an unusual double ring. It is found on roadsides, tracks and in urban areas.

Agaricus family
Cap size: 5–15 cm
Spore print colour:
Deep brown
Smell: Slightly sour
Season: Summer
and autumn

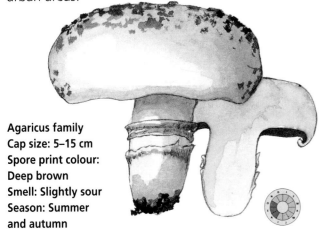

Coprinus comatus

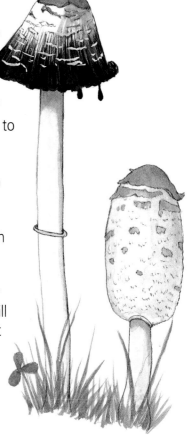

Its common names –
Lawyer's Wig or Shaggy Mane
– refer to the shaggy surface of the cap. Each scale curves back to look very like the curls on a lawyer's wig. The cap rapidly dissolves away from the margin and thus releases its spores. Search for it beside roads, in grass, freshly laid lawns, rubbish dumps and landfills. The 'ink' which drips from the cap has been used in times past literally as writing ink. Try it, but you will find without preservative that it rapidly turns smelly.

Coprinus family
Cap size: 5–10 cm
Spore print colour: Black
Smell: Pleasant
Season: Late summer and autumn

Agrocybe molesta

Here is a species that you may find in spring growing in open grassy areas or waste places such as roadsides. Check the whitish to pale tan cap which is often cracked. The white stem is smooth to fibrous with a narrow ring near the top.

Bolbitius family
Cap size: 5–7.5 cm
Spore print colour: Dull tobacco-brown
Smell: Mushroomy
Season: Spring to late summer

Aleuria aurantia

Commonly known as Orange Peel Fungus. As you walk along a woodland path or beside a bare soil path along a road, you may spot this species growing there. Often where it does occur, you will find it growing in large groups rather pressed together. The flesh is thin and brittle, tending to whiteness. The outside of this pretty fungus is covered with a soft pale down.

Cup fungus family
Fruit body size: 2.5–10 cm
Smell: Indistinct
Season: Autumn and early winter

Fungi at Home

Most kinds of fungi do not look interesting for long, once they are removed from the wild because they rot, so it is difficult to make a fungi collection that will last. But there are several ways of putting your favourite mushrooms on display at home. You can collect various bracket fungi (see page 7), or make models of the most attractive fungi that you see on your expeditions. Another way is to draw, paint, or photograph your favourite specimens. Here are a few ideas for you to try at home.

Making a fungi habitat

Another idea is to create a mini fungi habitat in a container at home. For this you will need some very fresh specimens. Many kinds of mushrooms will probably look attractive for a week or so, but do not expect them to last for much longer than this. Bracket fungi will last the longest.

1 **Take an old aquarium tank or a large plastic container** and put a layer of soil in the

Mushroom models

If you want a permanent model to keep at home, you can easily make one using modelling clay. Most mushrooms are simple in shape so they are easy to copy. Why not try making models of your favourite mushrooms that you have found on your expeditions?

1 **Buy some modelling clay** from your local art shop or stationer's.
2 **Choose a fungus** that you want to copy. Make sure that it is fresh, and make a note of its colours in your notebook.
3 **Now make your model.** You will probably need to make the cap and the stem separately. Take a ball of clay and squash it flat for the cap.

4 **Next roll out a sausage shape for the stem.** Don't forget to scratch in the gills, pores, or spines on the underside of the cap.

5 **When it is as lifelike as you can make it, leave your model to dry** for a day or two, until it is hard.
6 **Paint your model and try to match the colours** of the real fungus, including as many of the small details as possible. When the paint is dry, you may want to varnish it.
7 **Display your best models** by standing them in a little soil on a flat plate. Place some moss and dried leaves around their bases to make them look even more realistic.

bottom, about 5 cm thick. Lay a few pieces of moss, leaf litter and rotting bark on top.

2 **Collect some fungi** by lifting them out of the soil very gently with your trowel or teaspoon. Don't disturb the soil more than you must.

3 **Wrap them in paper and transport them home** in plastic containers like old yogurt pots or ice-cream tubs.

4 **Plant your specimens in the soil** very carefully.

5 **Wash your hands afterwards.**

6 **Keep the soil moist by spraying it** with a little water. If one of your specimens is growing on a piece of wood or a small log, you can keep it alive by spraying it with water.

7 **Don't try to add Stinkhorns** (see page 7) to your fungi habitat – they are much too smelly!

Grow mouldy

Mould is a kind of fungus. It spreads by spores, just like mushrooms do, and if the spores land in a suitable place that is damp and warm, mould will grow. Moulds are often very colourful and they are interesting to look at through a magnifying glass. Make notes of how fast it grows in your notebook.

1 **Take a slice of bread**, dampen it slightly with a little water, then put it in a clear plastic bag and leave it somewhere warm for a few days.

2 **After 2–3 days, the bread will start to look grey and furry in places**. These furry patches are where mould is beginning to grow.

3 **Use your lens to see the mould close up.** Don't open the bag, once the mould starts growing. Throw the bag away after a week.

4 **Try this experiment with a piece of fruit** like a plum or peach. Is the mould the same colour or is it different? If it looks green, it could be a species of mould called *Penicillium* which grows on rotting fruit. This is what the first antibiotic medicine, called Penicillin, was made from.

Parasites & Wood-rotters

Many fungi depend upon other plants or animals, either alive or dead, for their food and living space. They can be divided into parasites – which attack living things – and wood-rotters, which mostly feed on decaying things.

The wood-rotters play an important part in nature by turning dead wood into humus (the dark brown material formed when plants and animals decay). This humus is what the next generation of trees and plants will grow from. However, foresters dread an outbreak of the parasite, *Armillaria mellea* (see page 68), in their woods because it can destroy thousands of pounds worth of timber in a very short time. Some parasites will attack most trees; others only attack particular types of trees.

Many of these parasites live for years, particularly those from the Bracket Fungus family (see page 7). You can see them on trees at any time of the year, but the best time to see wood-rotters is in the autumn. In the spring and summer, look in fields for the fungi that grow from animal droppings.

The picture shows twenty-two fungi from the following section; see how many you can identify.

Armillaria mellea,
Auricularia auricula-judae,
Boletus parasiticus, Chondrostereum
purpureum, Coprinus atramentarius,
Coprinus micaceus, Fistula hepatica, Ganoderma
applanatum, Ganoderma lucidum, Gymnopilus
junonius, Hypholoma fasciculare, Hypholoma
sublateritium, Laetiporus sulphureus,Meripilus
giganteus, Mycena galericulata, Mycena haematopus, Paxillus
atrotomentosus, Pholiota aurivella, Pleurotus ostreatus,
Polyporus squamosus, Scutellina scutellata, Xylaria polymorpha.

Parasites & Wood-rotters

Armillaria lutea

Commonly known as the Honey Mushroom. You will recognize this species by its bulbous stem and reddish-brown to pinkish-brown cap which has brown scales at the centre. The gills range from cream to pinkish-buff. The stem is similarly coloured and often has a yellow coating near the base. Look especially for the white, cobwebby veil at the top of the stem. This fungus is often in large numbers scattered over a large area on buried wood or roots of dying trees.

Tricholoma family
Cap size: 5–10 cm – Spore print colour: White
Smell: Not distinct – Season: August-October

Collybia fusipes

Commonly known as Spindle Shanks. Search for this species growing in large clumps at the base of oaks and beeches. The unusual shape of the tough, fibrous and twisted stem should help you recognize it. The fleshy, smooth, domed caps are pale brick-red to reddish-buff and go darker with age. The flesh is white and tinged red-brown. It is a common species in southern England, but scarcer further north.

Tricholoma family
Cap size: 5–10 cm
Spore print colour: White
Smell: Slightly spicy
Season: Late spring until end of autumn

Boletus parasiticus

Here is a unique one for you to look for. It grows only on the fruit bodies of the Common Earthball (*Scleroderma citrinum*, see page 29). You may find a number of this parasite growing on the same host. Despite its invasion it seems to do no damage to the Earthball. It is a locally common species, especially in wet seasons.

Bolete family
Cap size: 2.5–7.5 cm – Spore print colour: Yellow-brown
Smell: Indistinct – Season: Autumn

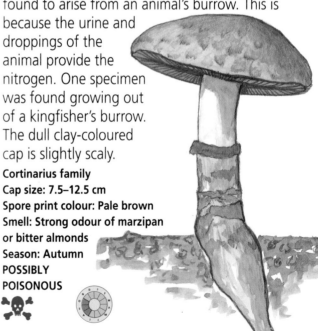

Hebeloma radicosum

This fascinating species has a unique lifestyle. It seems to require soil with a high nitrogen content in order to grow. If the long rooting stem is traced down through the soil it will almost certainly be found to arise from an animal's burrow. This is because the urine and droppings of the animal provide the nitrogen. One specimen was found growing out of a kingfisher's burrow. The dull clay-coloured cap is slightly scaly.

Cortinarius family
Cap size: 7.5–12.5 cm
Spore print colour: Pale brown
Smell: Strong odour of marzipan or bitter almonds
Season: Autumn
POSSIBLY POISONOUS

Fistulina hepatica

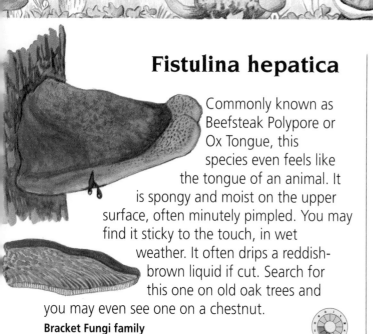

Commonly known as Beefsteak Polypore or Ox Tongue, this species even feels like the tongue of an animal. It is spongy and moist on the upper surface, often minutely pimpled. You may find it sticky to the touch, in wet weather. It often drips a reddish-brown liquid if cut. Search for this one on old oak trees and you may even see one on a chestnut.

Bracket Fungi family
Cap size: 7.5–25 cm – Spore print colour: Pinkish-salmon
Smell: Faintly pleasant – Season: Late summer and autumn

Ganoderma applanatum

Commonly known as Artist's Fungus (to discover why, see the Activity on page 51). This species forms large, very hard and woody brackets on dead and dying trees everywhere. The upper surface is hard and dry, crusty and lumpy and of a grey-brown colour. You might find it covered with a layer of bright rust-brown spores. The white pores on the underside will bruise brown if you touch them. New layers of tubes form each year and some of these fungi may be years old.

Bracket Fungi family
Cap size: 10–50 cm
Spore print colour: Reddish-brown
Smell: Mushrooms
Season: From May, it lasts several years

Ganoderma lucidum

Many fungi are being investigated for possible medicinal uses. Some are known to be antibiotic, others reduce cholesterol, or excessive fats in the blood, and a few may have anti-tumour potential for cancer treatment. This species is known for the latter. This fungus has a highly polished appearance from chestnut to reddish-purple and almost black. It is a common parasite on oak, chestnut and some other trees in the south.

Bracket Fungi family
Cap size: 10–25 cm – Spore print colour: Brown
Smell: Not distinct
Season: Throughout the year

Grifola frondosa

Commonly known as Hen of the Woods. Many bracket fungi seem to make use of wounds or injuries to a tree, to enter and infect it. They often fruit at the actual site of the injury. Hen of the Woods tends to fruit at the base of oak trees that have been struck by lightning. If you look closely above a group of this fungi you will see the long jagged wound caused by the strike. This species is formed of many caps all fused together.

Bracket Fungi family
Individual cap size: 2.5–7.5 cm
Entire fruit body: 15–50 cm
Spore print colour: White
Smell: Rather sour
Season: Autumn to winter

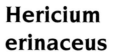

Pholiota aurivella

You should search for this species especially among beech trees. It usually grows out from an old decaying knot-hole or wound in the trunk and on fallen logs. The cap is bright orange and very slippery to the touch. It has jelly-like, dark brown scales which can wash off in wet weather. The stem is dry with small curved scales, below the ring. This ring disappears as the fungus grows older.

Stropharia family – Cap size: 5–15 cm
Spore print colour: Ochre-brown
Smell: Not distinct
Season: Autumn and early winter

Armillaria mellea

Commonly known as the Honey Mushroom. This is a serious parasite of woodland trees where it causes many millions of pounds' worth of damage each year worldwide. It also attacks many kinds of garden plants, especially shrubs. The caps vary from bright honey-yellow to greenish-yellow with a darker centre. The stems taper downwards. If you find some, peel back the bark of the dead or dying tree and you will see the tough black 'bootlaces' which are the means by which the fungus spreads long distances to infect other trees.

Tricholoma family
Cap size: 5–10 cm
Spore print colour: White
Smell: Unpleasant
Season: Summer, autumn and early winter

Hericium erinaceus

Commonly known as Hedgehog Fungus. This uncommon and spectacular fungus is a parasite growing high up on beech, oak or maple trees. It forms a compact mass with hanging spines several centimetres long. These spines are white when young, but discolour to yellowish with age. This is another species that has evolved to use spiny projections on which the spores are formed.

Toothed Fungi family
Cap size: 10–20 cm – Spore print colour: White
Smell: Indistinct – Season: Late summer and autumn

Chondrostereum purpureum

Commonly known as the Silver Leaf Fungus. You may find this fungus growing on a fruit tree in a garden. It favours apple, plum and cherry. As it infects the tree it forms a silvery blight on the leaves hence the common name. Unfortunately for gardeners, it usually kills the tree. The fungus appears as a crust, which spreads out to form small brackets. They have a lovely lavender-purple edge and undersurface. You will find the top surface hairy or woolly to touch. It is also found on woodland trees.

Crust Fungi family
Cap size: 10–15 cm – Spore print colour: White
Smell: Indistinct – Season: Throughout the year

Laetiporus sulphureus

Commonly known as the Chicken Mushroom. This brightly coloured species is a parasite on oak, chestnut and occasionally yew. It forms a series of overlapping brackets of bright yellow-orange. Some forms are pinkish-orange. You may find it growing at the base of trees or very high up. Some weigh several kilograms, and one large specimen required a wheelbarrow to transport it. In young specimens the flesh exudes a yellow juice if you squeeze it.

Bracket Fungi family
Cap size: 10–75 cm – Spore print colour: White
Smell: Not distinct – Season: Summer and autumn

Pholiota alnicola

A mushroom with a whitish-lavender veil which leaves tiny pieces hanging on the margin of the cap. There is a ring zone at the stem apex. You should search for this one around the base of dead trees, especially birch and alder. It grows in clumps and you could easily mistake it for the Sulphur Tuft Mushroom (*Hypholoma fasciculare*, see page 73). However, that species has purple-brown spores and is more fragile, while *Pholiota alnicola* has ochre-brown spores.

Stropharia family
Cap size: 5–10 cm
Spore print colour: Ochre-brown
Smell: Pleasant odour
Season: Autumn

Sparassis crispa

Commonly known as the Cauliflower Mushroom, this really looks like a cauliflower. It is formed of a large number of flattened, crispy lobes all twisted together. They grow out of a rooting base or stem buried deep in the ground. It is a weak parasite of conifers. Search for it around the base of standing trees or near stumps. It is not a common species so you may have to be patient before you see one.

Coral Fungi family
Cap size: 15–30 cm
Spore print colour: White
Smell: Spicy or cheesy
Season: Autumn

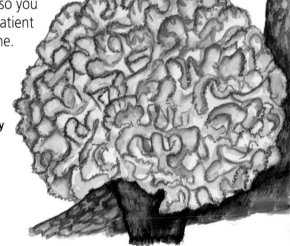

Meripilus giganteus

This bracket fungus is one of the largest you will ever see in this country. It is unmistakable with its enormous flattened and wavy caps. It grows from a base at the bottom of the tree gradually outwards to reach a mature size of nearly one metre. It is a parasite of oak and beech. All parts will bruise black if you handle it.

Bracket Fungi family
Cap size 25–75 cm
Spore print colour: White
Smell: Not distinct
Season: Autumn to early winter

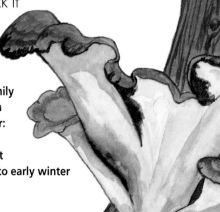

Mycena galericulata

Commonly known as the Bonnet Mycena. If you are a beginner fungus hunter you may find this one difficult to recognize. It grows in clusters in its habitat on broad-leaved tree stumps and fallen branches. You will find it deeply rooting into the wood. Look for the blunt, conical cap which is wrinkled and a dull grey-brown. White gills can be pink in older specimens. The shiny grey stems are fused into clumps and the flesh is white and thin.

Tricholoma family   Cap size: 2.5–5 cm
Spore print colour: White
Smell: Unpleasantly mealy
Season: All the year around

Xerula radicata

Commonly known as the Rooting Shank. While some fungi grow from wood on the surface of the soil, there are others, like this one, which prefer buried wood or tree roots. The stem grows into a long, deeply rooting taproot until it reaches a piece of wood. In some specimens you may be able to trace it down as much as 20 cm. The ochre-brown to buff cap is slippery to the touch in wet weather. The stem is scurfy in small tufts lower down.

Tricholoma family
Cap size: 5–12.5 cm
Spore print colour: White – Smell: Not distinct
Season: Summer and autumn

Mycena haematopus

Commonly known as the Bleeding Mycena, if you damage the stem of this fungus you may see it 'bleed' a dark reddish-brown juice. It is a wood-rotter and you should search for it on old stumps of broad-leaved trees. It has small bell-shaped caps coloured dark reddish-brown to wine-red with small teeth along the margin. It usually grows in clusters. Avoid contact with this juice because it will stain your fingers for some time.

Tricholoma family
Cap size: 1–5 cm – Spore print colour: White
Smell: Not distinctive – Season: Autumn

Mycena inclinata

You may easily confuse this species with *Mycena galericulata* (see left). The species shown here has minute, but distinct teeth around the margin of the bell-shaped cap. Use your hand-lens to look closely at the stem and you will see it is flecked with minute tufts of white cottony hairs. It is a wood rotter, and grows in small tufts on fallen logs and tree stumps. Search especially among oaks.

Tricholoma family
Cap size: 2.5–5 cm
Spore print colour: White
Smell: Unpleasant, soapy
Season: August until late autumn

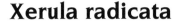

Cyathus striatus

Commonly known as the Bird's Nest Fungus. You will enjoy finding this tiny fungus. It is a locally common species which grows in woodlands. Search for it carefully among fallen twigs and branches. If you look within the bottom of the cup or nest you will see a few tiny, 1–2 mm, spore-bearing eggs. They are waiting to be splashed out and spread by raindrops.

Bird's Nest Fungi family
Fruit body size: 0.6–2 mm
Smell: Indistinct
Season: From spring
to autumn

Coprinus micaceus

A distinctive feature of this species is its cap. View it through your hand-lens and you will see a fine layer of shining reflective cells all over the reddish-brown surface. Also through a lens the stem is silky. Note that these white stems are joined together in large clusters. You will find it growing at the base of stumps and buried wood where it is a well-known wood-rotter.

Coprinus family
Cap size: 2.5–3.5 cm
Spore print colour:
Black
Smell: Not distinctive
Season: Late spring to
early winter
POSSIBLY POISONOUS

Pluteus cervinus

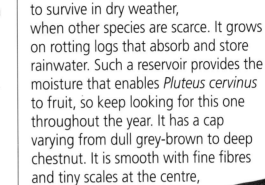

This species has developed a life style that enables it to survive in dry weather, when other species are scarce. It grows on rotting logs that absorb and store rainwater. Such a reservoir provides the moisture that enables *Pluteus cervinus* to fruit, so keep looking for this one throughout the year. It has a cap varying from dull grey-brown to deep chestnut. It is smooth with fine fibres and tiny scales at the centre, and has white gills.

Pluteus family
Cap size: 5–10 cm
Spore print colour: Pink – Smell: Not distinctive
Season: Throughout the year when conditions suitable

Paxillus atrotomentosus

This is another species that confines itself to a single type of tree. You will find it growing in tufts on the dead stumps of pine trees. The brownish cap is depressed in the centre, and the margin curved inwards. The off-centre stem is covered in buff down which becomes darker brown and velvety with age. The soft gills are yellow and the flesh yellow to pinkish. Be careful not to confuse this species with the poisonous *Paxillus involutus* (page 32).

Paxillus family
Cap size: 5–20 cm
Spore print colour: Yellowish-brown
Smell: Indistinct
Season: late summer to late autumn

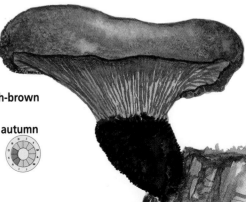

Flammulina velutipes

The weather factors that destroy most fungi are frosts or even cold weather for a prolonged period. However, this species is actually stimulated into growth and fruiting by low temperatures. So look for it between October and early spring. The caps are bright orange-yellow, smooth and sticky. The gills are a pale creamy–yellow. The slender, velvety, yellow stems become blackish below. Look for it on dead or dying timber.

Tricholoma family
Cap size: 2.5–7.5 cm
Spore print colour: White – Smell: Pleasant
Season: Late autumn to spring especially in freezing weather

Polyporus squamosus

The 'Dryad' of this mushroom's common name, the Dryad's Saddle, is a mythical wood nymph. This species grows into quite large bracket fungi and the pale ochre cap has bold, flattened dark brown scales. The short tough stem is black at its base. Search for it in deciduous woodland and you may find some growing out of standing or fallen timber. It is one of the first fungi to be seen in early summer.

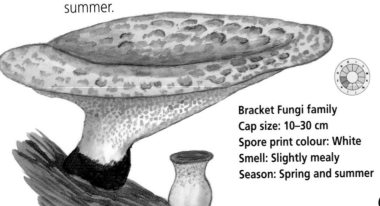

Bracket Fungi family
Cap size: 10–30 cm
Spore print colour: White
Smell: Slightly mealy
Season: Spring and summer

Calocera viscosa

At first sight you might think this is a coral or club fungus such as *Clavulinopsis fusiformis* (see page 56). But if you touch it you will feel the texture is rubbery and gelatinous, not brittle like a club fungus. In fact it is part of the Jelly Fungi family. You should be able to find it growing on dead coniferous wood. In very dry weather it may shrivel into a small, hard, dark orange lump.

Jelly Fungis family
Fruit body size: 2.5–10 cm
Spore print colour: Ochre-yellow
Smell: Not distinctive
Season: Autumn and winter

Tremella mesenterica

Commonly known as Witches' Butter, this fungus drapes itself in wrinkled folds from dead and rotting branches. It behaves in an unusual way too. When the weather turns dry, it shrinks into a hard, shrivelled lump. Then, when it rains, it revives into its bright yellow, white or transparent mass once more. If you feel it with your fingers you will find it flabby and jelly-like.

Jelly Fungi family
Fruit body size: 2.5–10 cm
Spore print colour: Yellowish
Smell: Indistinct
Season: All year. Search after rainy weather

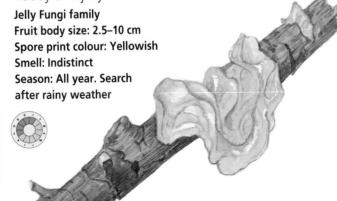

Hypholoma fasciculare

Commonly known as Sulphur Tuft. This species may be found in both wet and mild weather, almost any time of the year. It grows in tufts on fallen logs and stumps in both deciduous and coniferous woods. Since it is probably poisonous you should leave it untouched. The clustered caps are bright yellow-orange becoming pale sulphur-yellow with age. The stem has a faint ring zone, often more obvious when spores have fallen and collected around it.

Stropharia family – Cap size: 2.5–7.5 cm
Spore print colour: Purple-brown
Smell: None – Season: Autumn and winter
POSSIBLY POISONOUS

Hypholoma sublateritium

The common name, Brick Caps, refers to the brick-red cap with pale veil remnants at the margin. You should search for this fungus when the weather turns cooler at the end of the year. That is when it begins to fruit. The gills start whitish-yellow and then become grey-violet. The thick stem has a cobwebby veil near the top. It grows in tufts on fallen deciduous timber.

Stropharia family
Cap size: 5–10 cm
Spore print colour: Purple-brown
Smell: None
Season: Late summer and autumn

Gymnopilus junonius

This fungus is quite spectacular. If you search carefully through a woodland, you could find it growing in a large clump fixed to buried wood, on fallen logs and the stumps of deciduous trees. As it grows older the caps become coarse and fibrous and scaly. The orange to rust brown gills are often speckled. The stem is spindle-shaped or club-shaped.

Cortinarius family
Cap size: 7.5–15 cm
Spore print colour: Bright orange-brown
Smell: Not very distinctive
Season: Autumn

Piptoporus betulinus

Commonly known as Birch Polypore. This is a bracket fungus you should be able to find in almost any birch wood. It is a species that grows only on birch. People have found more uses for it than for any other fungus. It makes a good firelighter when dry, it has been used to sharpen old fashioned cut-throat razors and was once used like a styptic pencil to stop bleeding. Today, museums all over the world cut it into narrow strips to pin insects on display.

Bracket Fungi family – Cap size: 5–25 cm
Spore print colour: White – Smell: Pleasant
Season: It persists throughout the year. New growth in autumn

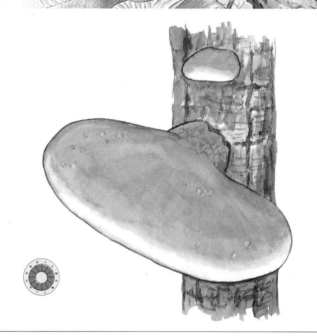

Oudemansiella mucida

Commonly known as Porcelain Fungus. One day as you walk through a wood you may be lucky enough to see a beech tree covered in massed drifts of the shining white caps of this fungus. It is one of the most sticky and slippery of fungi and has a thick layer of mucus on both cap and stem. It is used to produce an antibiotic called mucidin which reportedly helps in the cure of skin fungi like athletes' foot.

Tricholoma family
Cap size: 5–10 cm
Spore print colour: White
Smell: Indistinct
Season: Late summer to early winter

Volvariella bombycina

This large and beautiful mushroom is rather rare. Its host tree is the elm which recently has become the victim of Dutch Elm Disease. When the trees started dying, this fungus began to increase in numbers, growing in clusters in wounds and knot-holes on the decaying host. It begins life enclosed in an egg-like volval sac. You will find its remains at the base of the fruiting mushroom. The cap is white to slightly yellowish.

Pluteus family
Cap size: 5–15 cm
Spore print colour: Pink
Smell: Pleasant, but indistinct
Season: Early summer to end of autumn

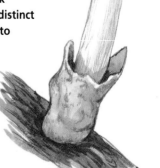

Xylaria hypoxylon

Can you see how this fungus gets its common names, Candle-snuff or Stag's Horn Fungus? It has a tough black stem often forking several times and which is white and powdery at the tips. If you collect one on the wood and keep it in darkness it will form long growths.

Flask Fungi family
Fruit body size: 2.5–8 cm
Spore print colour: Black
Smell: Indistinct
Season: All year

Xylaria polymorpha

This mushroom's gruesome common name, Dead Man's Fingers, refers to its shape. It grows in clumps of hard, black, bloated or misshapen 'fingers'. If you cut into it you will find the flesh is white. The spores are produced in tiny chambers in the tough skin. It is a typical wood-rotter and you will find it growing on old stumps or buried wood.

Flask Fungi family
Fruit body size: 5–10 cm
Spore print colour: Black
Smell: Indistinct
Season: All year around

Cyathus olla

At first glance this fungus looks rather like the Bird's Nest Fungus (*Cyathus striatus*, see page 71). But if you look closely you will find the 'nests' of this species are tiny, flared funnels. Their inner surfaces are smooth and white to pale grey. The eggs are whitish-grey. Raindrops propel the eggs out of the cup. Search for it on open arable land, fields, pastures, sand-dunes and on woody debris.

Bird's Nest Fungi family
Fruit body size: 0.6–1 cm
Smell: Indistinct – Season: Spring to autumn

Scutellinia scutellata

This is a tiny species for you to look at in close-up with your hand-lens. The margins of the bright deep scarlet cups are fringed with a single row of black eyelash-like hairs. Look beneath it to see the minute hairs covering the underside of the cap. You will find it in the forest if you look really closely at wet, rotted logs. It is common everywhere.

Cup Fungi family
Fruit body size: 0.6-1 cm
Smell: None noticeable
Season: Late spring, summer and autumn

Pleurotus ostreatus

Commonly known as the Oyster Cap, this is a species that is now cultivated commercially and is available from many food stores. The caps usually have no stem and grow directly out of dead or dying timber and are deep bluish-grey to grey-brown. The narrow and crowded gills are white to greyish. You should be able to find it growing in enormous numbers late in the year from both standing and fallen trees.

Pleurotus family
Cap size: 5–15 cm – Spore print colour: Pale lilac
Smell: Pleasant – Season: Late in the year

Megacollybia platyphylla

This is one for you to look for early in the year, especially after late spring rain, but it continues to fruit until autumn. The dull grey to grey-brown cap is smooth with fine fibres. But you will most likely recognize it by its gills. They are white and widely spaced with the edges often split or jagged. It is extremely common and often the only species to be found fruiting in a woodland in summer, on logs, stumps and buried wood.

Tricholoma family
Cap size: 5-15 cm
Spore print colour: White
Smell: Not distinctive
Season: Summer and autumn

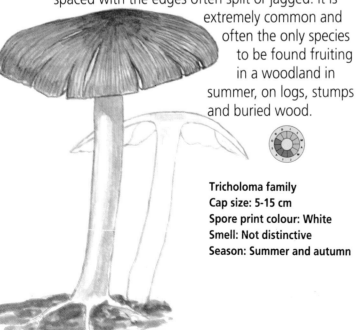

Coprinus atramentarius

Known as the Common Ink Cap, this species favours a habitat with stumps and buried wood where it grows in large clumps. Like other Ink Caps (*Coprinus* family), it drips black ink. Its cap is grey-brown, slightly scaly with spindle-shaped stem with a ring zone close to the base. Be careful with this one because it is regarded as possibly poisonous, so it is better for you to look and leave well alone.

Coprinus family
Cap size: 2.5–5 cm
Spore print colour: Black
Smell: Not distinctive
Season: Early summer and autumn
POSSIBLY POISONOUS ☠

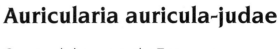

Stereum hirsutum

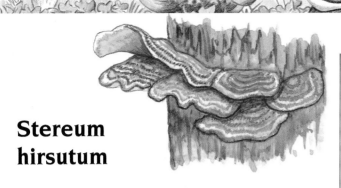

In this species you will find many individual caps overlapping each other to form a large mass. Sometimes they fuse together. The upper surface is zoned in shades of grey, white or brown. If you look closely with your hand-lens you will see it is finely hairy or velvety. The undersurface is smooth yellow-grey. It grows mostly on fallen timber of birch and beech as well as other deciduous timber.

Crust Fungi family
Cap size: 1–2.5 cm – Spore print colour: White
Smell: none noticeable – Season: Throughout the year

Auricularia auricula-judae

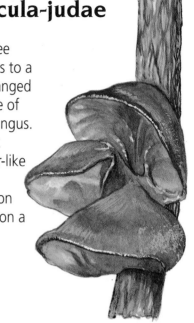

Commonly known as the Tree Ear, this fungus's name refers to a legend that Judas Iscariot hanged himself on an elder tree, one of the favourite hosts of this fungus. It is supposed to be his spirit appearing in this strange ear-like form. These 'ears' are softly rubbery and slightly velvety on the outside. In fact it grows on a variety of host trees.

Tree Ear Fungi family
Fruit body size: 2.5–15 cm
Spore print colour: White
Smell: Not distinctive
Season: All year round

Daedaliopsis confragosa

You should be able to find this species on various types of dead wood where it often persists for several years. The caps are semi-circular, tough and fibrous, grey-brown with both paler and darker zones. If you cut it you will find the flesh whitish, then pinkish and finally pale brown. Its pores are very variable. They can be round to elongated or even gill-like, but all of them will bruise pinkish when handled.

Bracket Fungi family
Cap size: 5–10 cm
Spore print colour: White
Smell: None distinguishable
Season: Throughout the year

Trametes versicolor

This is one of the commonest and most well-known of the Bracket Fungi. Search in any woodland and you should be able to find it growing on logs, stumps and rotting branches of deciduous trees. You might even find it on stored logs. Each bracket is zoned with an amazing variety of colours from brown to grey, blue-black, yellow, green and purple. Often you will find old specimens from the previous year.

Bracket Fungi family
Cap size: 2.5–10 cm – Spore print colour: White
Smell: Indistinct – Season: All the year round

Find Out Some More

Useful organizations

The best organization for you to get in touch with is your local County Wildlife Trust. There are forty-seven of these trusts in Great Britain and you should contact them if you want to know about wildlife and nature reserves in your area. Ask your local library for their address, or contact:

The Wildlife Trusts (formerly Royal Society for Nature Conservation), The Green, Witham Park, Waterside South, Lincoln LN5 7JR (01522–544400).

Wildlife Watch is the junior branch of The Wildlife Trusts. Local Wildlife Watch groups run meetings all over the country. You can find out about your nearest group by contacting The Wildlife Trusts.

The British Mycological Society is a nationwide and overseas group for both experts and beginners. They publish a bulletin with some articles aimed at children. They also organize Fungus Forays. Contact Dr G W Beakes (Membership Secretary), PO Box 30, Stourbridge, West Midlands DY9 9PZ.

Your local **natural history society** may organize walks to find and study mushrooms. They are led by local experts and you will find them a great help. There may also be a local natural history group you could contact. Your local library will have a list of such societies.

Birmingham Natural History Society, 58 Edgbaston Park Road, Birmingham B15 2RT. This society is particularly interested in studying fungi.

The Nature Conservancy Council, Calthorpe House, Calthorpe Street, Banbury, Oxon OX16 8EX. Write to them for a list of local Nature Reserves. Try and persuade your parents to take you to some Nature Reserves – many of them have Interpretive Centres to explain the wildlife present there. They should also have information on unusual fungi on the reserve. However you **must not** collect on Nature Reserves.

National Trust for Places of Historic Interest or Natural Beauty, 36 Queen Anne's Gate, London SW1H 9AS (0171–222 9251). They own more than 570 properties and over 232,000 hectares of unspoiled countryside throughout England, Wales and Northern Ireland, including over 850 kilometres of coastline. They run many courses for school groups; ask your teacher to find out about these.

In Scotland, contact **The National Trust for Scotland** (care of the Education Adviser), 5 Charlotte Square, Edinburgh EH2 4DU (0131–226 5922).

Useful books

There are many illustrated field guides that will help you find and identify mushrooms in Great Britain and Ireland. Look for one with clear illustrations.

Collins Guide to Mushrooms and Toadstools by S. Buczacki (HarperCollins, 1993).

Fungi and Lichens by Wendy Madgwick (Heinemann, 1990). An illustrated guide to the biology and ecology of mushrooms, and their environmental and ecological importance.

An Illustrated Guide to Mushrooms and Other Fungi of Britain and Northern Europe by Geoffrey Kibby (Dragon's World, 1992). A large guide to over 400 species of fungi, ranging from the common to the very rare.

Kingfisher Field Guide to the Mushrooms & Toadstools of Britain & Europe by D. Pegler (Kingfisher, 1990).

Mushrooms and Toadstools by Derek Reid (Kingfisher, 1980). An illustrated guide to common mushrooms and toadstools.

The Pocket Guide to Mushrooms and Other Fungi by Geoffrey Kibby (Dragon's World, 1992). A handy, spiral-bound field guide to mushrooms and other fungi of Britain and Europe.

Index & Glossary

To find the name of a fungus in this index, search under its main name. So, to look up *Fistulina hepatica*; look under *Fistulina*, not under *hepatica*.

A

Agaricus arvensis 55
Agaricus bitorquis 61
Agaricus campestris 55
Agaricus silvaticus 46
Agaricus xanthodermus 59
Agrocybe molesta 61
Aleuria aurantia 61
Amanita citrina 18
Amanita fulva 13
Amanita muscaria 33
Amanita pantherina 13
Amanita phalloides 26
Amanita porphyria 15
Amanita rubescens 12
Amanita spissa 15
Amanita strobiliformis 40
Armillaria lutea 66
Armillaria mellea 68
Auricularia auricula-judae 77
Auriscalpium vulgare 46

B

Bolbitius vitellinus 57
Boletus aereus 30
Boletus appendiculatus 30
Boletus badius 10
Boletus calopus 17
Boletus chrysenteron 10
Boletus edulis 10
Boletus erythropus 10
Boletus luridus 29
Boletus parasiticus 66
Boletus piperatus 11
Boletus pruinatus 36
Boletus rubellus 31
Boletus satanus 31
Boletus subtomentosus 29
boss the dome in the centre of a fungi's cap, also called the *umbo* 27
Bovista plumbea 56

C

Calocera viscosa 72
Calocybe gambosum 59
Cantharellus cibarius 18
Cantharellus tubaeformis 21
Chondrostereum purpureum 68
Chroogomphus rutilus 49
Clavariadelphus pistillaris 40
Clavulina cristata 18
Clavulinopsis fusiformis 56
Clitocybe clavipes 47
Clitocybe geotropa 28
Clitocybe nebularis 27
Clitocybe nuda 58
Clitocybe odora 16
Clitopilus prunulus 16
Collybia butyracea 12
Collybia dryophila 19
Collybia fusipes 66
Collybia maculata 19
coniferous describing trees with needles instead of leaves, like pines 12

Places to visit:

You will find fungi growing wherever you go, even in your back garden. If you walk through your local woods in Autumn, you should see a variety of fungi. Find out from the **Forestry Commission**, Public Information Division, 231 Corstorphine Road, Edinburgh EH12 7AT (031-334 0303) where your local woodlands and forests are.

Although there are no reserves set aside for fungi in particular, many **nature reserves** (see opposite) throughout the country have lists of the fungi found there and protect them along with other wildlife. Some of the sand dune areas along Britain's coastline are rich habitats for fungi, many are found nowhere else. Note that reserves usually have very strict policies about not picking.

The Royal Botanic Garden, Edinburgh has a fungus garden where a changing display of actual growing fungi can be seen.

Coprinus atramentarius 76
Coprinus comatus 61
Coprinus micaceus 70
Coprinus picaceus 40
Cortinarius alboviolaceus 38
Cortinarius armillatus 37
Cortinarius bolaris 39
Cortinarius pseudosalor 37
Cortinarius purpurascens 14
Cortinarius semisanguineus 13
Cortinarius traganus 45
Cortinarius trivialis 20
Craterellus cornucopiodes 38
Cyathus olla 75
Cyathus striatus 71
Cystolepiota aspera 37
Cystolepiota bucknallii 26

D

Daedaliopsis confragosa 77
deciduous describing trees that lose their leaves in the autumn. Most are broad-leaf, like beeches or oaks 12

E

Entoloma incanum 54
Entoloma nidorosum 21

F

Fistulina hepatica 67
Flammulina velutipes 72
fruiting body the bit of the fungus that appears above ground, which scatters the spores 6

79

Index & Glossary

Endorsed by Wildlife Watch:

Wildlife Watch is the national wildlife and environmental club for young people. It is the junior section of The Wildlife Trusts, the largest voluntary organization in the United Kingdom, which is dedicated to protecting our wildlife and wild places.

Wildlife Watch groups throughout the United Kingdom take part in exciting national projects and play an active role in nature conservation. Wildlife Watch members receive the club magazine WATCHWORD three times a year. It is packed full with ideas, projects and articles explaining current environmental concerns.

For further information, please send a stamped addressed envelope to the address below.

**The Green,
Witham Park
Waterside South
Lincoln LN5 7JR**